THE *BetterWay* TO

Create BABY SCRAPBOOKS

THE *BetterWay* TO

Create BABY SCRAPBOOKS

by the editors of *Memory Makers* magazine

**IDEAS, TIPS AND TECHNIQUES
FOR BABY SCRAPBOOKS**

BETTERWAY BOOKS
Cincinnati, Ohio

PROJECT DIRECTORS	Michele & Ron Gerbrandt
EDITORIAL DIRECTOR	MaryJo Regier
ART DIRECTOR	Sylvie Abecassis
CRAFT DIRECTOR	Pam Klassen
IDEA COORDINATOR	Pennie Stutzman
CONTRIBUTING WRITERS	Jennifer W. Johnson, Margaret Radford, Anne Wilbur
CRAFT ARTIST	Erikia Ghumm
GRAPHIC DESIGNER	Susha Roberts
PRODUCTION	Diane Gibbs, Nicole King, Rudy Landry, Virginia MacKinnon
EDITORIAL SUPPORT	Dena Twinem, Carolyn Newman
LETTERING ARTISTS	Jennifer T. Johnson, Sharon Kropp, Virginia Russell, Mary-Kay Tilden-Dyck, Emily Tucker
PHOTOGRAPHY	Cambon Photography Satellite Press — Ken Trujillo

Published by Betterway Books, an imprint of F+W Publications, Inc.
4700 East Galbraith Road, Cincinnati, OH 45236
Phone 1-800-289-0963
First edition. Manufactured in the United States of America.

08 07 06 05 04   5 4 3 2 1

A catalog record for this book is available from the Library of Congress
at http://catalog.loc.gov.

Memory Makers Books is the home of *Memory Makers*, the scrapbook magazine dedicated to educating
and inspiring scrapbookers. To subscribe, or for more information, call 1-800-366-6465.
Visit us on the Internet at www.memorymakersmagazine.com

Contents

p.60

p.94

p.52

sasha, 6 mos.

anna, 6 mos.

Introduction

Of all the scrapbooks we are most likely to create, baby scrapbooks are among the most popular. When newborns enter our life, whether we're a parent, a grandparent or an aunt, they capture our hearts with deep emotion and unconditional love. Creating their baby scrapbook documents a piece of their life that they won't remember. It shows them they were loved and cared for, and points out personality traits that they've carried since birth.

Through my own three children, I have witnessed how swiftly their first year passes. And through the countless baby scrapbook pages graciously sent in by our readers, I've been able to share in the joyous celebrations of new life and all that babies bring to our lives and families. I hope you enjoy this same heartwarming experience as you look through the pages of this book.

We have featured many distinctive ideas. In addition, we tell the stories behind the pages. Included are page ideas for pregnancy, showers, name selection, birth, family and more. We also included adoption, ceremony and cultural pages, as well as treatments for portraits and heritage pages. And since a baby's daily activities are the equivalent of a parents' workday, we've paid extra attention to those all-important sleepytime, bathtime, mealtime, illnesses and boo-boos, playtime and growth pages. Lastly, we have included historical and informative baby-related sidebars and tips.

michele and sasha, 1994

Baby's first year bustles with rapid growth and wondrous change. Few parents can resist capturing their wide-eyed innocence, toothless grins and miraculous "firsts" in photos. And with an estimated 4 million babies born each year, we're talking about a lot of photos.

Whether you're new to scrapbooking or a seasoned veteran, a grandparent or a parent-to-be, there is inspiration here for everyone.

Michele

DANIEL
(SEE PAGE 126)

FOUNDER OF MEMORY MAKERS® MAGAZINE

Checklists

Like most parents, you will take a lot of photos and you will save everything!
Use these lists as the basic framework for organizing your photos and memorabilia.

BABY PHOTOS

☐ Positive pregnancy test
☐ Stages of pregnancy
☐ Mom receiving ultrasound
☐ Nursery preparation
☐ Baby shower guests, gifts, refreshments
☐ Hospital and hospital nursery
☐ Actual birth or adoption
☐ Doctor's and nurses' care
☐ Baby with doctor or midwife
☐ First time Mom and Dad hold baby
☐ Baby meets siblings and family
☐ Baby's tiny fingers and toes
☐ Leaving hospital and homecoming
☐ Baptism, christening, ceremonies
☐ Baby in baby equipment

☐ Sleeping and favorite blanket
☐ Nursing and mealtime
☐ Bathtime
☐ Playtime and favorite toys
☐ Monthly growth
☐ Baby with favorite stuffed animal each month
☐ Monthly weigh-ins and shots
☐ Milestones and firsts (see page 97)
☐ Funny faces
☐ Holidays
☐ Illnesses and boo-boos
☐ Baby with family pets
☐ Travel and outings
☐ Professional portraits

JOURNALING

Try to keep a daily journal
that chronicles pregnancy, birth,
the adoption process and life with baby.
If there's no time for journaling, jot tiny notes on
a calendar to add to the scrapbook later.
Other things you might wish to record:
☐ *Reactions to news of pregnancy*
☐ *Pre-birth letter to Baby*
☐ *Name selection process*
☐ *Family tree with personal histories*
☐ *Trip to hospital*
☐ *Story of labor*
☐ *Timed contractions*
☐ *Names and comments of doctor and nurses*
☐ *Post-birth letters to Baby*
☐ *Beloved lullabies, poems, quotes and games*
☐ *Relationships with special people*
☐ *Milestones and firsts (see page 97)*
☐ *Baby's unique habits*

MEMORABILIA

☐ Baby's ultrasound photos
☐ Color-copied nursery wallpaper/fabric swatches
☐ Shower invitations and cards
☐ Squares cut from shower wrapping papers
☐ Gift list and registry
☐ Hospital bracelets, bassinet name tag
☐ Umbilical cord and circumcision rings
☐ Hospital and doctor bills
☐ Copy of doctor's notes
☐ Copy of birth certificate
☐ Foot and hand prints
☐ Birth announcement
☐ Newspaper clippings (see page 58, de-acidifying)
☐ Church bulletin announcements
☐ Congratulatory cards
☐ E-mail announcement and replies
☐ Letters to Baby from family and friends
☐ Ceremony mementos
☐ Baby photos of Mom and Dad
☐ Heritage baby photos of relatives
☐ Time capsule souvenirs
☐ Formula, food and diaper labels
☐ Growth and development records
☐ First lock of hair

Scrapbook Supplies

Use these lists of basic tools and supplies and unique design additions to help you get started on your baby scrapbook album.

BASIC TOOLS & SUPPLIES

Albums & Scrapbook Pages
Colored and Printed Papers
Page Protectors
Pens and Markers
Permanent and Removable Adhesives
Ruler
Scissors

UNIQUE DESIGN ADDITIONS

Die Cuts
Fancy Rulers
Fancy Scissors
Journaling and Design Templates
Memorabilia Pockets
Paper Frames
Paper Trimmers/Cutters
Photo Corners
Punches
Stamps
Stickers

For preservation purposes, we strongly recommend the use of acid- and lignin-free albums and paper products, photo-safe adhesives, PVC-free plastics and pigment inks.

Children
are the
heart of
the family

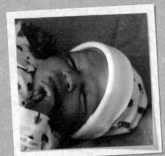

Mommy
Daddy
and
Sawyer
1998

CHILDREN ARE...
ALEX BISHOP
HANDMADE SCRAPS
FARMINGTON, UTAH
(SEE PAGE 126)

Getting Started

Infancy is fast-paced and filled with tender and meaningful moments. Moments that few parents, friends and relatives can resist capturing in photographs. While the thought of creating a baby scrapbook album may seem overwhelming, a little pre-planning, organization and inspiration will make the labor of love manageable and rewarding.

1 ORGANIZE PHOTOS AND MEMORABILIA

Use checklists on page 8 as a guide for organizing your photos and memorabilia. Jot down memories that your photos inspire which may have been neglected through journaling. Sort according to events or chronological order, determining if you will add pre-birth photos and memorabilia into the album. You may want to enlarge some photos. Assembling sorted photos and memorabilia to be included in the album will help determine the album's size, number of pages and page protectors needed.

2 ALBUM SELECTION

Albums come in three-ring binder, spiral, post bound or strap-style. The most popular, readily available sizes are 12 x 12" and 8½ x 11". Sturdy albums will withstand the test of time. Albums should provide an acid- and lignin-free and photo-safe environment for photos and memorabilia. Expandable albums are best for making baby's album an ongoing project.

3 VISUAL THEME SELECTION

Your baby album's visual theme will depend on your photos and memorabilia, as well as what fits your style and budget. The repeated use of a design element, color or unique border can give the album continuity. Shop with a list of page layouts and some photos to avoid any unnecessary spending.

4 CREATING LAYOUTS

Composition
Beautiful scrapbook pages and albums rely on balanced, eye-pleasing composition. For example, the page to the right is simple yet balanced. Consider using two-page spreads that are clean and basic as opposed to making each page a unique work of art. Save elaborate designs and fancy techniques for title pages and important photographs. Some basic concepts to help your page composition follow. And remember, layout an entire page or spread before mounting anything.

Focal Point
A scrapbook page may contain several photos, but one should be important enough to be a focal point. Use the rest of the page and photos to complement the focal point.

Creative Photo Cropping
Creative cropping breaks the monotony of a square or rectangular page while emphasizing the subject or removing busy backgrounds. You will find many successful examples of photo cropping throughout the pages of this book.

rhys, 9 mos.

Matting and Framing

You can focus attention on special photos with decorative mats and frames, which can be purchased or handmade with colored or printed papers, fancy scissors and templates. Selected colors should complement photos without stealing away any attention.

Adding Embellishments

Once your photos and memorabilia are in place, complete the layout by adding design embellishments such as stickers, die cuts, punched shapes and more.

5 JOURNALING

No page is complete without your own words to tell the story. Handwritten words add a personal touch. There are also computer fonts, lettering books and journaling templates available. We have also included lettering patterns and page title ideas (see pages 122-123) to help you. Try to tell your baby's story without relying solely on photos. Our journaling checklist (see page 8) will help bring your photographic story to life.

Morgan, Jackson, Aidan & Brendan
The Kelly Quadruplets
7 months old

Three Page Designs

We invited three artists to take a scrapbook challenge. In addition to a packet of the same scrapbook supplies (shown right), we also gave the three scrapbookers a set of photos of these cute quadruplets, provided by their mother, Tricia Kelly of Thousand Oaks, California. We then challenged the artists to unleash their personalities and imaginations on a baby scrapbook page.

While the three page designs are quite different, they all possess unique personality and imagination. And that's what scrapbooking is all about!

See page 126 for the materials included in the packets sent to the three artists.

Hug Please

TRY A SIMPLE BORDER PAGE

Michele's quick, basic design covers a 12 x 12" scrapbook page. She chose to use four individual portraits in an effort to capture the quadruplets as individuals. Note how Michele colored the stamped babies' outfits blue and pink, just as the real babies are dressed in the photos. Her easy, four-corner border, simple journaling and simple photo treatments also help keep the focus of attention on the photos themselves.

Michele Rank, Cerritos, California

Hug Me 1st, 2nd, 3rd and 4th!

TIE IT ALL TOGETHER WITH RIBBON

Linda's intermediate design incorporates silk ribbon, torn paper and miniature silk ribbon rosettes to help mimic the softness of the photos on this 12 x 15" scrapbook page. She has put her stamped babies with tiny strips of ribbon inside 3-D Keepers™ for the future addition of locks of hair from each baby.

Linda Strauss, Provo, Utah

Special Request, Please Open...

MAKE AN INTERACTIVE DRESSER

Efrat's advanced design showcases a whimsical, three-dimensional motif across a two-page, 8½ x 11" spread. The pop-ups and pull-outs emphasize the whirl of activity that there certainly must be with four babies in one house. Silhouette cut photos, stickers and the addition of magazine cutouts add to the unique personality of Efrat's design.

Efrat Dalton, Fort Collins, Colorado

Oh happy day!

On March 9, 1999, after 2 home pregnancy tests came out positive, (Tammy wasn't convinced the first time.) we learned we were expecting a baby! We caught the exciting moment with the self-timer on our camera. A visit to the doctor the following day confirmed the results of the tests.

jack, newborn

wes, newborn

Getting Ready

A NEW BABY IS LIKE THE

BEGINNING OF ALL THINGS —

WONDER, HOPE, A

DREAM OF POSSIBILITIES

— *EDA J. LE SHAN*

We learn in an instant that a child is coming, but we believe it only in baby steps. The first flush of morning sickness. The little "swish-swish" of Baby's heart on the sonogram. When we search our souls for the name we've always known. Preparing for a baby means making room in your home and in your heart. But it will pass in the blink of an eye, so record it now. Save those ultrasound and pregnancy photos, shower cards and nursery fabric swatches. Record your emotions and life dreams, for they are about to come true.

emily, newborn

OH HAPPY DAY!
TAMARA SHIROMA
KAPOLEI, HAWAII
(SEE PAGE 126)

Lauren's Nursery

MATCH NURSERY DECOR

Sticker borders and stamped letters highlight photos of Cheri's garden-theme nursery. Start by layering photos on pale green parchment. For the title, stamp the beginning letters (Stampin' Up!) with green ink on gold paper; cut out and border with green dots. Stamp remaining letters directly on the background. Adhere fence, flower, leaf, butterfly and green line stickers (Frances Meyer). Stamp red ladybugs (Stampin' Up!).

Cheri O'Donnell, Orange, California

Marie's Story

While awaiting the arrival of their first child, David and Shawnee settled on a jungle theme for baby Alexis' nursery. David asked his mom, amateur artist Marie, to design a wall mural featuring jungle animals. Years earlier, Marie had painted David's childhood room with his beloved Fantastic Four® comic book characters.

After sketching the design in pencil on the bedroom wall, Marie put everyone in the family to work. "At first they were all scared to death that they would ruin the painting," says Marie. "But with a little encouragement, the mural slowly came to life."

The family painted lions, zebras, giraffes, elephants, monkeys, parrots and hippos, which Marie later re-created for a pop-up page in her scrapbook. Shawnee's favorite animals are rabbits, which you don't usually find in the tropics.

"Of course there aren't any rabbits in the jungle," laughs Marie. "But our mural indeed has rabbits sitting on top of a giraffe."

By the end of the day all of the novice painters commented on how well they did. Their self-affirmation didn't surprise Marie one bit. "I believe we all have artistic ability," she says. "That ability just needs cultivating."

Marie Valentino, Happy Scrappin'
Shelton, Washington

See page 72 for instructions on how to make a bathtime pop-up.

paige, 3 mos.

Showered With Gifts

PHOTOGRAPH GIFTS

When Juanita adopted her daughter, she was showered with generosity. First, print title letters on blue paper. Cut each letter into a water droplet shape and mount along top borders. Print colored umbrellas (Sierra On-Line); mount along bottom borders. Silhouette cut and layer photos of baby gifts.

Juanita Yager, Gurnee, Illinois

UNIQUE BABY SHOWER GAMES

BINGO *Bingo with baby words instead of numbers.*

CREATE-A-CAPTION *Guests write captions for funny expressions of baby photos torn from magazines.*

DECORATE ONESIES *Guests decorate gift onesies with paints.*

DRESS BABY *Teams dress baby dolls fast and accurately.*

FILL BABY'S PIGGYBANK *Guests add pocket change to piggybank when "off limit" words or actions are exposed.*

GIFT BINGO *Bingo played during gift opening with gift words.*

GUESS THE BABY *Match each guest to his or her baby photo.*

IT'S IN THE BASKET *Display basket filled with baby items for 20 seconds; hide. Guests try to remember basket's contents.*

NAME GAME *Forming words with letters in Baby's name.*

OFF LIMITS *Certain action or word "off limits" during shower.*

RICE BOWL *Find safety pins in bowl of rice while blindfolded.*

ROUND-THE-TUMMY *Guests estimate size of Mommy's tummy with lengths of string or toilet paper.*

SCRAPBOOK *Guests make baby pages for Mommy to add photos to; guests write notes to Mommy and Baby.*

SHOWER-IN-A-BOX *Out-of-town relatives and friends participate in gift-giving by mail; opening of gifts is videotaped or photographed and sent to "guests" with thank-you notes.*

STORY-GO-ROUND *Start baby story with "Once Upon a Time..." Each guest adds to story; see what develops by "The End."*

TIME CAPSULE *Guests bring contemporary items to encapsulate for Baby to open some day.*

WHISPER CHAIN *One guest whispers baby advice to another guest. See how good the advice is once it has come "full circle."*

Baby Shower

FILL A PUNCH ART UMBRELLA

Basic punches add quick decorations to Kim's festive umbrella. Use umbrella stencil (Puzzle Mates) to create umbrella from printed paper. Trim photos to fit umbrella. Cut rectangles for gift boxes. Trim strips for ribbons and freehand cut polka dot bow. For gingham bow, punch two medium hearts and a small circle. For polka dot flowers, punch medium flowers and $\frac{1}{4}$" circles. For edge of umbrella, punch medium flowers, small circles and mini swirls. Freehand cut lavender and silver handle.

Kim Heffington, Avondale, Arizona

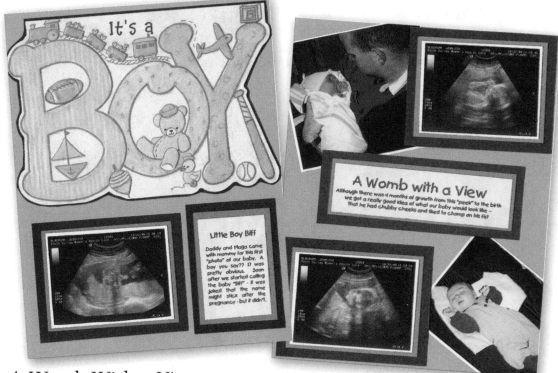

A Womb With a View

MATCH BEFORE/AFTER PHOTOS

The ultrasound of Jennifer's son not only showed that he was a boy but also that he had chubby cheeks and liked to suck on his fist. After he was born, she took pictures of him in similar positions. To create this fun layout, use a blue or pink background. Double mat printed journaling (DJ Inkers) and ultrasound photos. Single mat photos and greeting card.

Jennifer Blackham, West Jordan, Utah

BABY DOLLS

Hand cut babies from printed paper; assemble. Add ¼" punched circles for cheeks and punched mini heart on dress; draw details.

Michelle Lizz King, Ceres, California

BABY'S DEVELOPMENT

From conception to delivery, Baby's miraculous growth is fun to follow.

1ST MONTH *Baby is a tiny, tadpole-like embryo, smaller than a grain of rice.*

2ND MONTH *Baby looks more human as facial features, fingers, toes, eyes and ears begin to develop.*

3RD MONTH *Baby is now 2½ to 4" long and weighs about ½ ounce. Organs are developing, including reproductive organs. Gender is still hard to detect.*

4TH MONTH *At 4 to 6" in length, baby nourishes from the placenta and is developing reflexes. Tooth buds, nails, hair, eyebrows, eyelids and eyelashes are forming.*

5TH MONTH *Mommy begins to feel movements of her 8 to 10" baby. Lanugo and vernix cover its body, hair begins to grow on its head and brows and white eyelashes appear.*

6TH MONTH *Baby weighs about 1¾ pounds and is about 13" long. All essential organs are formed.*

7TH MONTH *Three-pound Baby can now suck its thumb, hiccup and even cry. It can taste sweet or sour and responds to pain, light and sound.*

8TH MONTH *At 18" long and 5 pounds in weight, active Baby can now see and hear. Brain growth is tremendous but lungs are still immature.*

9TH MONTH *Weighing about 7 pounds and about 20" in length, Baby becomes less active in its confines as it prepares for birth.*

joshua, 2 mos.

carlos, 3 weeks

LET'S GO TO THE VIDEOTAPE

"When Stephen was born, we didn't have a good camera or any good shots of him as a newborn," says Anne Heyen of Glendale, New York. "So we photographed shots from his video on the television screen with a new point-and-shoot camera from 4-5 feet away."

The Incredible Expanding Woman

SHOW PREGNANCY'S PROGRESSION

During four months of bed rest, the only time Cheri got "made up" was for these monthly photos. After collecting a pregnancy photo series, use a balloon template (Extra Special Products) to trim photos into balloon shapes. Silhouette a head photo and mount above pregnant body die cut (Accu-Cut). Journal and draw details with colored pens. Adhere heart and angel stickers (source unknown) on die cut.

Cheri O'Donnell, Orange, California

Life on the Inside

PROFILE A PRECIOUS PRISONER

The ID number for Melissa's "prisoner" was her daughter's actual birth date printed in the Brittanic Bold font (Sierra On-Line). To make the striped background, cut ½" white strips and space ½" apart on black paper. Write the birth story using a humorous "prison record" style. Print the title and story. Mat all elements with black paper.

Melissa Jordan, Cassville, New York

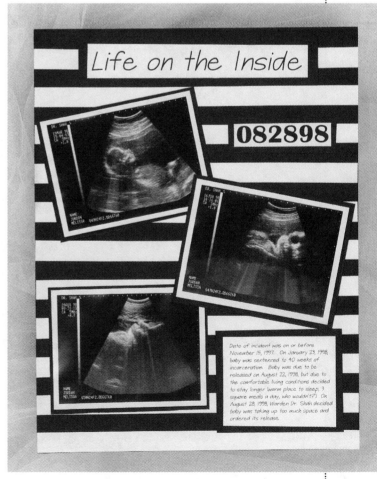

Expectation...

We found out that we would be blessed with a second child on Thanksgiving day! Well that's definitely something to be thankful for...

A new chapter in our lives is about to begin. We are both a little afraid...both excited...both wondering about the changes a new life will bring to our family...

Bethany is thrilled to find out there will be a little brother or sister joining her... She's telling everyone she is going to have a baby. She says there is a baby in her tummy too!

Nine months suddenly seems like such a short time to prepare...There is so much that needs to be done, and yet nine months seems almost an eternity to wait...What does this new baby look like? What kind of child will it be? The heart is already beating inside me, I am in awe of the precious gift that is growing inside my body...

Wonderment, Joy...

Expectation

REFLECT ON FUTURE BIRTH

Using a greeting card illustration, Dale wrote simply and beautifully about the joy and wonderment of expecting her second child. For the titles and first letters of each paragraph, use a thick blue calligraphy pen. Journal and draw embellishments using thin blue, green and pink pens.

Dale Caliaro, Oviedo, Florida

NAMING BABY

Naming Baby is a thoughtful and enlightened process. With heritage, cultural and religious considerations to ponder, as well as distinction, style and character attributes, the evolution of the naming process will continue to change over time.

TEN MOST POPULAR BABY NAMES...THEN AND NOW*

1899		1999	
MALE	FEMALE	MALE	FEMALE
1. John	Mary	1. Michael	Emily
2. William	Anna	2. Jacob	Samantha
3. George	Margaret	3. Matthew	Madison
4. James	Helen	4. Christopher	Ashley
5. Joseph	Marie	5. Joshua	Sarah
6. Charles	Elizabeth	6. Austin	Hannah
7. Frank	Florence	7. Nicholas	Jessica
8. Robert	Ruth	8. Tyler	Alyssa
9. Henry	Ethel	9. Joseph	Alexis
10. Edward	Alice	10. Andrew	Kayla

*From the Social Security Administration's Office of the Chief Actuary

annelise, newborn

YOUR NAME

You got it from your father,
It was all he had to give.
So it's yours to use and cherish
For as long as you may live.

If you lose the watch he gave you,
It can always be replaced.
But a black mark on your name, son,
Can never be erased.

It was clean the day you took it,
And a worthy name to bear.
When he got it from his father,
There was no dishonor there.

So make sure you guard it wisely,
After all is said and done.
You'll be glad the name is spotless
When you give it to your son.

-Author Unknown

FAVORITE GIRL NAMES

Stasha
Calah
Gabriel
Danielle
Grae

What's in a name?

Sasha,

When you were born, your father and I weren't certain of a name. We were fond of "Calah" and "Stasha" but after you came, the names just didn't fit. But you did look like a "Sasha," with your dark hair and strength of body.

I prayed for God to reveal a name and that night I dreamed of the name, "Sasha Kiev." Kiev? What was that about? I told your Dad about my dream. He discovered that Kiev was the capital of the Ukraine (where some of my long-ago ancestors were born) and that the Mennonites passed through Kiev while escaping Russia during the Mennonite persecution. "Kiev" relates to both sides of our family!

Sasha (a form of Alexander) Kiev. And your middle name goes well with your sister, Anna Kiah and with Dad's, Ronald Keith. It's a strong Russian name and the family thought we were crazy. But Sasha Kiev Gerbrandt seemed just perfect! You will always be our little Sasha.

FAVORITE BOY NAMES

Daniel
Jacob
Gabriel
Joshua
Cael
Grae

Getting Closer

Daniel Cael
Daniel Jacob
Stasha Rene
Sasha Joelle

June 16, 1993

Sasha Kiev

TELL THE NAMING STORY

This page not only recalls the process of choosing Sasha's name but also lists Mom's and Dad's favorite names. First print the "What's in a name?" story directly on cream paper. Trace printed titles onto lavender paper using a purple pen. Mat story, photos and titles. Arrange elements on page and write favorite names. Freehand cut pink roses and lavender ribbons; punch small and mini swirls for centers. Use the swirl border punch #2 (Family Treasures) for the leaves.

Michele Gerbrandt, Memory Makers

INTRODUCING...

BAYLESS FARMS
organically grown

FIVE MAGIC BEANS
NET WT 10 g

MAY FLOWERS
FILL YOUR HEART
WITH A FRESH
PERSPECTIVE
AND NEW LIFE!

OUR FAMILY HAS
GROWN...
AND WE HAVE A NEW
SPROUT!

JACK CONNOR
WEGE BAYLESS

SPROUTED
MAY 5, 1999
9:55 AM
HT. 23 1/2 INCHES
WT. 10LBS. 3 OZS.

PROUD PARENTS

SCOTT AND KATY
BAYLESS

Magic Beans   (HYBRED)

Children are like seeds, in each
there is a promise of the future.
Nurture them with love.

type	inches	grows best	days to germinate
annual	23½"	full sun	280

PLANTING INSTRUCTIONS

Sow in fertile soil giving lots of love
and affection. Water and feed often.
After becoming well established,
harvest after 18-21 years. Comes
from good stock.

kendall drue, 3 days

tori, newborn

Birth

WHEN OUR BABY STIRS AND

STRUGGLES TO BE BORN, IT

COMPELS HUMILITY: WHAT WE

BEGAN IS NOW ITS OWN.

— *ANNE RIDLER*

As Baby makes his or her debut, thinking gives way to doing as new life springs forth. And trusted people are there to help. Your spouse, partner, doctor or midwife. Maybe older children. Try to dictate labor milestones for your partner to record. Maybe allow photos from discreet angles. Bask in the moment your child's eyes first meet yours. Then gather up everything: hospital bracelets, APGAR scores, headlines from the day's newspaper and announcements to help make these fleeing moments last on a scrapbook page.

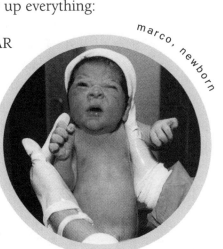
marco, newborn

INTRODUCING JACK BAYLESS
KATY BAYLESS
ALHAMBRA, CALIFORNIA
(SEE PAGE 126)

Ellis Levi Ackerman stepped into our lives on February 11th, 1999 at 5:14 in the morning

It's a Boy!

CREATE A PHOTO MOSAIC

As a neonatal nurse practitioner, Debra witnessed her grandchild's birth and performed his first physical exam. Her photo mosaic is the perfect way to document a fast-paced day. Titled by stickers (Mrs. Grossman's) and printed journaling, Debra's photo mosaic blends ten separate photos. Begin by using a ruler and pencil to lightly mark the horizontal and vertical cutting lines (to create 1" squares) on the back of the photo. Number the back of each square photo piece in chronological order to make reassembly easier. Slice photos vertically and horizontally on cutting lines using a small paper cutter. Piece together mosaic.

Debra Rodney, Tucson, Arizona

Special Delivery

POSTMARK THE NEW ARRIVAL

An old envelope provided the template for Arlene's pocket. Print the postmark onto solid blue paper using PrintShop Deluxe software (Broderbund). Mat with blue gingham. Unseal an envelope and trace the edges onto gingham paper; cut out, fold and seal. Arrange photo, printed journaling and stamped footprint encased in memorabilia pocket (3L Corp.) in envelope. Adhere "It's a Boy!" sticker (Frances Meyer).

Arlene Santos, Mililani, Hawaii

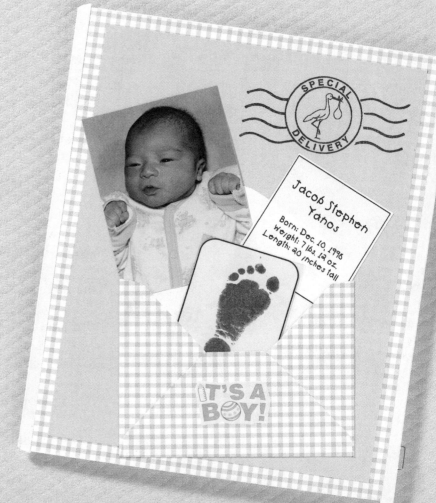

Mom & Dad's Hospital Band

Tyler's Hospital Band

Tylers Hospital Cap

1999

Coins

Tyler's Birth

DISPLAY 3-D MEMORABILIA

To protect the items related to her son's birth, Taniesa used 3-D Keepers™ (C-Thru Ruler Co.). These ¼" thick clear plastic boxes provide a sturdy home for just about any semi-flat object. Mount decorative paper beneath the boxes to help memorabilia stand out. To copy the star design, punch swirls and medium and small stars from printed paper. Draw details with silver pen. Print and mat titles. Double mat photo. Arrange elements on a dusty blue background.

Taniesa Thompson, Gilroy, California

Worth the Wait

SHOW DELIVERY BY THE CLOCK

Billie waited nine months and spent two days in labor to see her newborn son, a feat she documents in timely fashion. To make a similar page, cut a 7" black circle and a 6¼" white circle for clock face. Mount with freehand cut stem and hands; set time to your delivery time. Add cropped and silhouetted photos. Adhere number, letter and nursery stickers (Creative Memories). Finish with journaling.

Billie Martin, Seffner, Florida

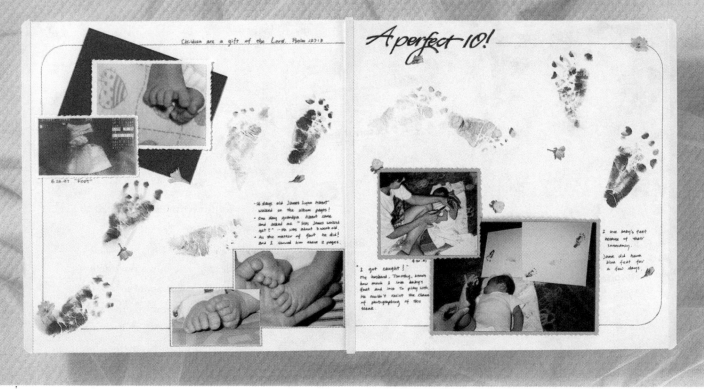

A Perfect 10!

STAMP PRECIOUS FOOTPRINTS

Hyeran's son had blue feet for a few days after "walking" on her page. She suggests that an easy way to stamp baby footprints is to first tape the paper to sturdy cardboard. Then, holding the ankle firmly, tap an ink pad onto baby's foot. Carefully stamp the footprint by pressing the paper against the foot. For the layout, first crop and mat photos. Draw title with a thick black pen. Draw thin black border lines, drawing corner curves using a small round object. Adhere rose stickers (Mrs. Grossman's). Journal with black pen.

Hyeran Albert, Martinez, California

Splashing Good News!

TUCK CARDS IN A PEEK-A-BOO POCKET

A duck shape is perfect for Tracy's country-style pocket page. First adhere a strip of gingham paper along the

top of the background page. Draw a curved wavy line along the top of a separate page and cut away the top portion to create top of pocket. Punch ¼" holes along the wavy edge. Weave two lengths of yellow ribbon through the holes, starting from the outside edges, and tie a bow. Trace an enlarged duck die cut (Ellison) onto the pocket and cut out, creating the "peek-a-boo" opening. Adhere the pocket to the background page along the left, bottom and right sides. Using a wavy ruler, mount a wavy gingham strip along the bottom edge of the pocket. Punch small yellow ducks.

Tracy Haynes, Boynton Beach, Florida

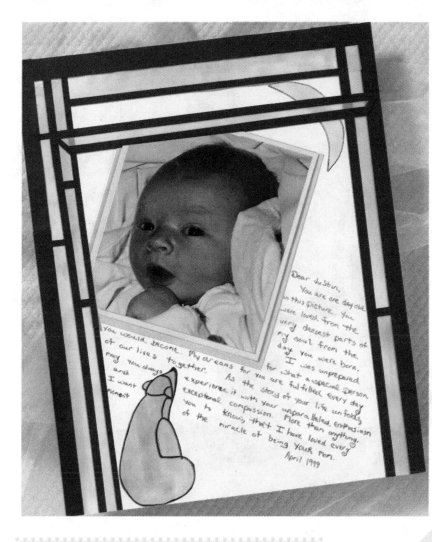

Love Letter

PIECE A STAINED-GLASS FRAME

Karen's stained-glass technique provides a lovely frame for her one-day-old son. Start by cutting a vellum crescent for the moon. Trace a bear design onto vellum using a black pen. Color the backs of these elements with chalk. Outline the moon with black pen. To create the stained-glass window frame, cut vellum and black strips. Color one side of the vellum strips with colored chalks. Layer the vellum strips beneath black strips. Double mat photo and trim corners. Write a love letter to the newborn; adhere.

Karen Wilson-Bonner, Tapestry in Time,
Livermore, California

BRIDE'S HANKY BABY BONNET

"My son, Ethan, wore a 'Bride's Hanky' bonnet home from the hospital," says Donna Hasker, of Temple Hills, Maryland. "One day his bride can remove the stitches and use it on her wedding day."

TIPS FOR BETTER BABY PHOTOS

Babies are popular photographic subjects. For the best baby photos follow these simple tips:

- *Keep camera loaded and handy.*
- *Use the right film speed (400 inside, 200 outside).*
- *Hold camera steady.*
- *Experiment with soft, available lighting and no flash.*
- *Use flash in low light and to fill shadows.*
- *Back-lighting can silhouette baby or highlight hair.*
- *Side-lighting illuminates baby's profile.*
- *Get in close to eliminate busy backgrounds.*
- *Take both horizontal and vertical photos.*
- *Frame baby off-center.*
- *Get down to baby's level to capture perspective.*
- *Try black and white film; it's forgiving of skin blemishes.*
- *Thumb through magazines for photo inspiration.*

TORN PAPER STORK
Linda Strauss, Provo, Utah

My Doctor

TAKE CAMERA TO CHECKUPS

Kathleen created a "photo-safe" bandage for the right photo by cutting it from printed paper (Hot Off The Press). Mat photos using torn mulberry paper and green card stock. Trim titles with decorative scissors. Journal with brown pen on white paper; mat with cream paper. Arrange elements on marble paper (Hot Off The Press).

Kathleen Fritz, St. Charles, Missouri

E-mail

SAVE COMPUTER GREETINGS

Congratulatory e-mails from friends and family fill Bamber's bright pocket. First mount printed paper (NRN Designs) on background page. Using a dinner plate, mark a cutting line on the top edge of the pocket; trim with decorative scissors. Adhere pocket to background page. Mount letter die cuts (Creative Memories). Adhere heart, square, circle and line stickers (Mrs. Grossman's). Trim printed e-mails with decorative scissors. Journal with red pen.

Bamber Grady, Fort Hood, Texas

PUNCH ART

Punch art is easy. All you need are a few punches and some paper to create captivating art from simple, punched paper shapes. Punch art adds charm and whimsy to scrapbook pages. It can also extend your scrapbooking budget by making good use of paper scraps that might otherwise be thrown away.

Punch art truly offers versatility and endless possibilities. There are two more cute examples of baby punch art on page 62. And for more baby-related punch art, see *Memory Makers Punch Your Art Out Volumes 1 & 2*. (See page 127 for ordering information.)

Our Baby

MAKE PUNCH ART ALPHABET BABY BLOCKS

Anissa's punch art alphabet baby blocks accent a simple page spread of unrelated baby photos. To make this spread, mount mint green matted photos on a forest green background. Punch 1" squares (Family Treasures) for blocks from mint green paper. For babies, punch ⅝" or small circles for heads and shoulders, ¼" round hand punch for hands and pacifiers and ⅛" round hand punch for ears, cheeks and pacifier grips and ¼" swirls (Family Treasures) for hair; assemble and adhere to blocks (see below). Finish with punched letters (Family Treasures), pen stroke stitching on blocks and photo mats and face details.

Anissa Stringer, Port Ludlow, Washington

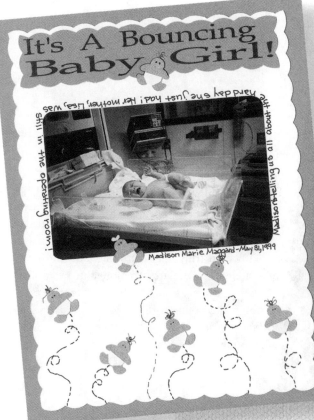

It's a Bouncing Baby Girl!

PUNCH TINY DIAPERED NEWBORNS

Julie's first granddaughter inspired these whimsical babies made with a teddy bear punch. For the background, trim white paper with large scallop scissors and layer on blue or pink. Print title and trim with scallop scissors. Round photo corners. Punch bears from flesh-colored paper, trimming off the ears. Punch an equal number of white bears, trimming into diaper shapes. Arrange babies with diapers. Draw dashed curly black lines and pink bows if desired.

Julie Bahr, Blue Springs, Missouri

News on the Day Gigi Arrived

EDIT PERSONALIZED FRONT PAGE

Joyce cut and pasted articles summarizing current events on the day her daughter was born. To make her own front page, Joyce started with a headline cut from a local paper. Cut out and arrange different articles, including the birth announcement if available. Photocopy and reduce onto white paper. For the page background, trim right edge of mauve paper using a scallop ruler to draw the cutting line. Punch small hearts. Joyce then color copied and enlarged the Diaperene® logo baby; cut out and layer with newspaper.

Joyce Schweitzer, Greensboro, North Carolina

mercedes, 5 mos.

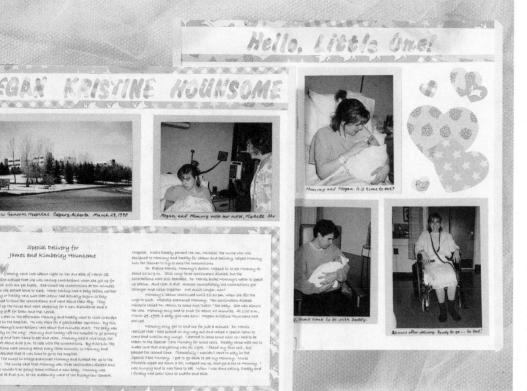

Megan Kristine Hounsome

JOURNAL ABOUT BIRTH

To make the title, Kimberley printed the letters on white paper using the Challenge Extra Bold font (Microsoft). Then she traced the letters onto the wrong side of printed paper (Frances Meyer) and cut them out with cuticle scissors. To complete the layout, cut matching strips of printed paper to border the title letters. Mat photos and the printed birth story. Write photo captions.

Kimberley Hounsome
Calgary, Alberta, Canada

Krista's Story

A mother-to-be's worst fears came true for Krista when her water broke prematurely during her 19th week of pregnancy. During several uneasy weeks of waiting, hoping and praying, the baby maintained stability. But when Krista began having contractions, the doctors sadly informed her that their fourth child was no longer showing a heartbeat and would be stillborn. The family was devastated.

Krista found that making a scrapbook page about Elizabeth helped her in her journey of grief. "I wanted a page to honor her brief time with our family and that the kids could look at when they feel like seeing her or talking about her," says Krista. Some of Elizabeth's mementos, however, were too painful to include in the album.

Krista finds the pages are a good way to talk with others about Elizabeth. She especially appreciates the times when neighbors or family see Elizabeth's tribute. "It makes me feel better that someone is interested in her," says Krista.

Krista Lee Feairheller, Kettering, Ohio

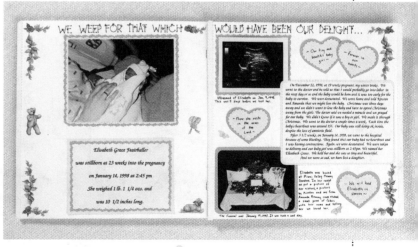

Punch Art Album

Amy Talarico, Northglenn, Colorado

Punch art offers a world of endless possibilities for baby scrapbook albums. The album that Amy created for her daughter is a gorgeous testament to the dimensional simplicity of baby punch art.

Amy had a Lucy Rigg™ baby book, which she adored. However, she wanted to create a scrapbook album that would last forever, complete with page protectors. Her solution was to combine elements from the Lucy Rigg book with her own scrapbook and punch art talents to create a truly unique baby scrapbook album.

Coming Home

The day and date Monday, December 29, 1996
Who came to take you home Grandma Haliw & Aunt Diane Haliw
Where your family lived at the time we lived with Grandma
Haliw at 2305 W. 92nd Ave. #111 in a trailer
Who was waiting to greet you Aunt Kristy Haliw, Cousin Tobi
Haliw, and Uncle Bob Haliw's girlfriend Natalie Kaylor.
How your room was decorated you shared a room with
mom. It was small but it was ours.

Amy's consistent use of a few simple punches and decorative scissors, combined with soft pastel papers and extensive journaling, give the album its classic appeal.

Amy spent untold hours creating the punch art and placing it carefully on the pages. Her album is a record of important facts, private thoughts and warmest feelings about her daughter. The result is a scrapbook album that gives her daughter the knowledge of how her birth and early years were truly anticipated and enjoyed.

Adoption

Adoptive families make memories that are unique to their experience: fragments of the search for their child, word of the baby's birth, details about the child's native country or biological family. All are vital to record, for adopted children will ask questions one day that your baby scrapbook album may help answer.

WE'RE HOME!

Frank & Maureen Robertazzi's 22-hour flight from China to New Jersey with their newly adopted baby landed at night, resulting in dark, unappealing photos. To enhance the photo of Aubri looking out the plane window, Frank removed the dark background by adding a digital photo of New York City at sunset. "It's the greatest city in the world," says Frank.

Maureen Robertazzi, East Hanover, New Jersey

Sharon's Story

Sharon stood in the middle of the Haitian orphanage surveying over 80 children. She felt overwhelmed by the inquiries posed. "Will you be my mama?" and "Can I go live with you in Canada?" With a husband and three boys waiting anxiously for her at home, Sharon wondered how she could possibly choose the right children to adopt.

"I wanted to take them all," says Sharon. "But I knew I couldn't." She eventually narrowed her picks down to a two-year-old girl and a pudgy baby boy. All too soon after the selection came a tearful goodbye, with promises to the two children that they could come live with their new family soon.

Daniel and Amanda finally arrived to a joyous welcome from their new family following 17 months of seemingly endless waiting. After watching her older boys treat the newcomers like guests for months, Sharon was actually relieved the first time she heard all of the kids squabbling. "Any mother gets tired of her children fighting," says Sharon. "But this time I thought, 'Oh! We're finally a family.'"

Sharon Fehr, Fort St. John, British Columbia, Canada

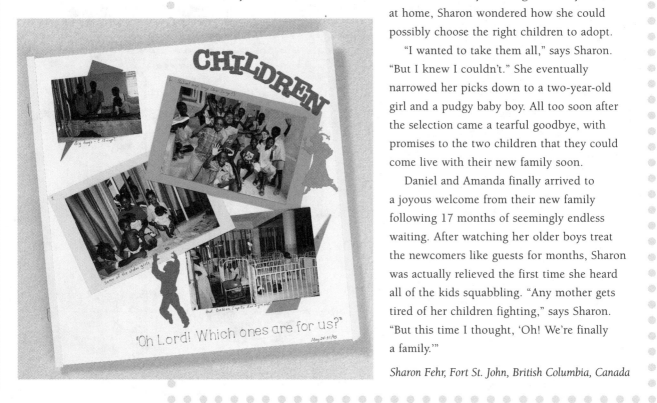

tucker, 7 mos.

Babies Are Heaven Sent

PRESERVE ADOPTION ANNOUNCEMENT

Chris begins baby Joey's adoption story with a simple page showcasing his announcement card. Mount yellow triangles on page. Adhere announcement and cropped photo. Embellish with stickers (Mrs. Grossman's, Sandylion).

Chris Peters, Hasbrouck Heights, New Jersey

Adoption

WRITE A THOUGHTFUL ACRONYM

This layout honors Michele's best friend, Becky Homan, who adopted twin girls born prematurely. Start by mounting the adoption announcement across the center of the layout. Mat photos and printed journaling using soft colors and decorative scissors. Adhere baby booties die cut (Making Memories) and small punched bears. Color in printed letter outlines for the word "adoption" with colored pencils.

Michele Lea, Oxford, Ohio

Adoption Album

Melanie Penry Mitchell, Overland Park, Kansas

Scrapbooks have proven to be an important tool for teaching adopted children about their past and their path, as they became part of a new family. Melanie's special album tells the story of the journey to adopt Mary, a Chinese baby girl, from start to finish: the ocean of paperwork, the months of waiting, packing for the trip to Beijing, sightseeing in China before getting Mary and meeting friends and family back in the United States.

Another fun and unique aspect of Melanie's album is her rebus journaling on the clothing page. It successfully documents the layers and layers of clothing Mary was wrapped in on the day of her adoption—a good idea since the adoption director asked for all of the clothes back except for the quilted suit seen in the center photo.

Hectic Day!

We walked in a garden 🌿 outside while **Daddy** took care of the paperwork. You **CRIED** till I thought 👀 to give you a c🍪🍪kie & Cheeri◯'s. You had a big steamed roll when you came in but you REALLY liked the cookie! 😊 I changed your diaper – **BOY** – were you wearing a lot of **CLOTHES** I really didn't know how many till I **UNPEELED** you back at the hotel. You were all hardly anything These the you **ALL at the time!** They made you were **WARM**! the little quilted suit ⬆ but the director asked for the others back. I wrote ✍ down what they looked like so we could **Remember.** I'm glad I did because so much happened that day! The **Registrar** asked us **Why** we wanted to adopt you – that was **EASY!** Daddy & I gave our fingerprints in RED INK. You gave your footprint 👣 which made you cry again. We took the bus to the **NOTARY'S** office – which was **FANCIER** but that's a **BLUR** because you woke up & were **SCARED** and I worried about you. *You were fine later that day!*

were clothes wore same sure We still have

- yellow knitted hat with cute little ears
- embroidered red velveteen vest
- this wash ▲ cloth was your bib tucked under your little chin
- padded yellow print pants with the Chinese split seat
- matching print jacket
- pink t-shirt type knit pants with the split seat
- knitted hot pink long-johns with the split seat
- two identical knitted sweaters that made you look like a little tiger
- long sleeved red & white polka-dot T-shirt
- plain white T-shirt
- diaper blue & white cloth
- 3 pairs of socks!
- red padded booties that tied around the ankles

Heading home part II

These are your **DOCUMENTS.** The **RED** one is your Passport that had the problem. The **Yellow** is your vaccination record. The **BROWN** is our Adoption document.

We pushed (& I mean PUSHED!) our way through Security & were ready to board our pla...

U.S. Immigration & Naturalization Service

Sarah Metzger

JEANNETTE L. CHU
OFFICER-IN-CHARGE

U. S. CONSULATE GENERAL
No. 1 Shamian South Street
Guangzhou, China 510133

TEL: 86-20-81888611
FAX: 86-20-81864001

It's Official!!

They called us back & looked over our paperwork. We expected an "interview" but all they asked was if we had moved since we applied. A little small talk & then Ta-Da!~You were Ours Forever! YIPPEE!!!

This is one of my FAVORITE PICTURES! You look so cute & happy!

Melanie employs hand-lettered journaling, great photos and lots of memorabilia throughout the album for a truly personal touch. And Mary, now 3, loves to look at her memory book. "You can never fill in all the blanks for adopted children, but it's important for her to know what a great experience it was to become a family," says Melanie. "We wouldn't have traded it for anything."

When You Wish Upon a Star Your Dreams Come True!

We wished, hoped, prayed & dreamed but never realized what a wonderful child you would be & how much we would fall in love with you!

...journey for you many years ago~ We didn't know then that we had to wait for you to be born~ But you were worth the wait!

happy, exhausted family

We travelled around the world on an extraordinary trip we'll never forget...

...to bring you home and make us a family forever and ever.

A baby's body is a joy and delight in his parents arms

Maron

Jan 1997

...ie and nathan, newborn

akemi and alexis, 1 mo.

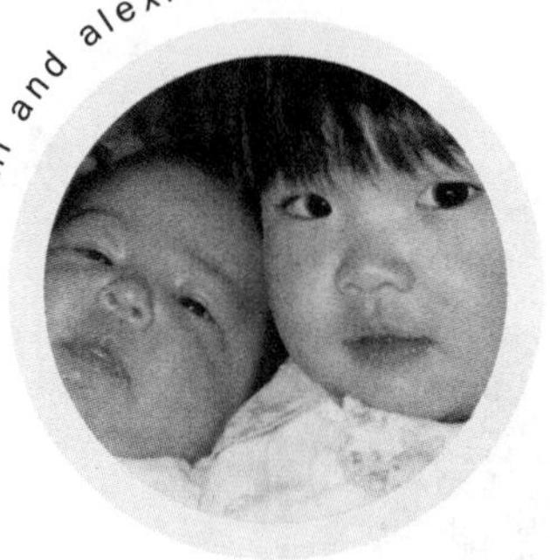

Family

A BABY IS GOD'S OPINION THAT LIFE SHOULD GO ON.

— *CARL SANDBURG*

A baby's urgent cries and blissful smiles enliven our spirits and renew our family bonds. What was once a collection of individuals with singular needs now becomes a unified circle of caregivers. This warmth and unity of purpose changes families forever. Mark it with photographs of those first feedings with Grandma, sibling interactions and precious snuggles with Daddy. A handwritten sample of your baby's sleep schedule and a list of first-time visitors will also make great additions to Baby's scrapbook album.

bryan, jessica and nile, 3 mos.

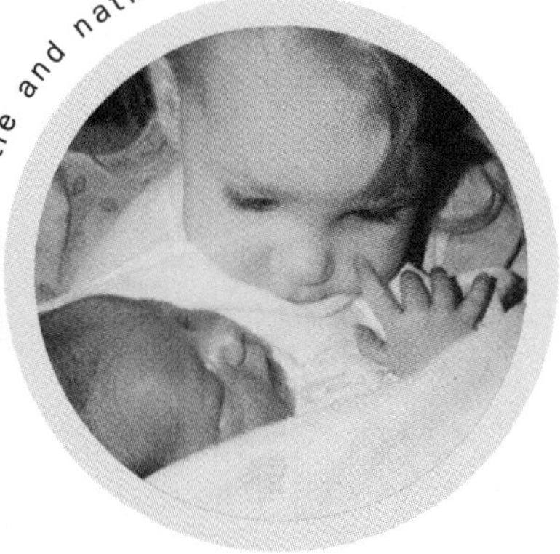

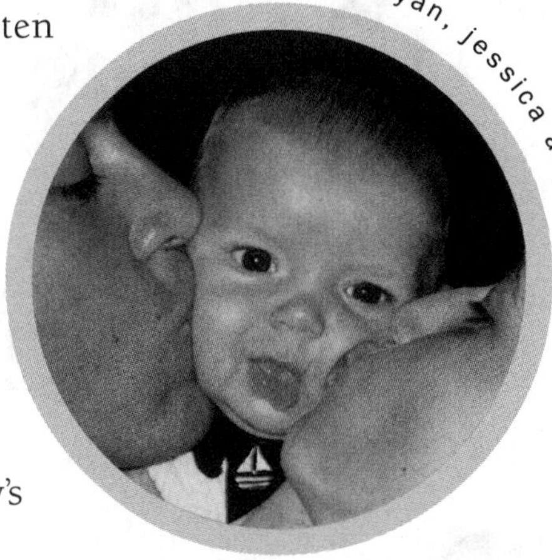

A BABY'S BODY...
DEANNA HAMMER
KELOWNA, BRITISH
COLUMBIA, CANADA
(SEE PAGE 126)

Sarah and Grandma

The dusty colors of Liza's layout create a gentle setting. Start with pale yellow for the page background. For top border, trim edges of blue strips using the Teardrop Corner Lace Edge punch (Family Treasures) with the guides removed. For title, adhere outlines of letter stickers (Creative Memories) to floral photos; cut out each letter leaving a 1/16" border. Crop and mat photos using the Teardrop Corner Lace Edge and corner rounder punches. Mat oval for journaling. Cut and layer pieces for baby in high chair. Journal with black pen.

Liza Wasinger, Fairfax, Virginia

Cathryn's Story

Cathryn was returning to work following the birth of daughter Natalie and required child care for her baby and older son, Win. Luckily, Cathryn's niece Alice desired to attend the junior college near her home. Alice found a home, and Cathryn a trusted caregiver for her children.

The house was soon filled with Natalie's squeals as she played with Alice. "I could see them forging a very sweet bond," remembers Cathryn. Alice's fiance, Aaron, and twin brother, Jake, joined her in doting on Natalie.

Cathryn's scrapbooking supplies frequently engulfed the living room table, so it wasn't long before Alice was hooked on the hobby.

Alice also provided Cathryn with welcome diversions. "We painted our toenails purple and bought toe rings, danced to Janet Jackson and watched 'Road Rules' on MTV," says Cathryn. "For me it was a yearlong slumber party."

Alice now attends San Francisco State and doesn't get to see the family as much. When she does get to visit, Natalie joyfully runs to the door calling for her cousin 'La La'.

Cathryn Vance, Santa Rosa, California

alexis, 13 mos.

katelyn, 4 mos.

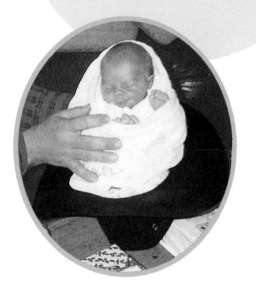

Austen and Mommy

COMBINE COLOR WITH BLACK-AND-WHITE

Cindy's color photos and classic black-and-whites capture the timelessness of a mother's love. For the background, adhere border stickers (Mrs. Grossman's) on light khaki card stock. Cut a sheet of soft plum paper in half diagonally to form triangles. Crop and mat photos using decorative scissors and templates. Double mat title using deckle scissors and corner rounder punch. Accent title with small flower sticker (Mrs. Grossman's).

Cindy Mandernach, Fraser, Michigan

Austen and Mommy frolicking in the beautiful sunshine
Heritage Park
August

I Love My Aunts

REMEMBER LOVING RELATIVES

Kelley took the time to photograph her baby with five doting aunts for this special scrapbook page. To copy the look, start with floral background (Frances Meyer). Crop photos and trim corners using Nostalgia corner scissors (Fiskars). Mat photos with striped paper (Hallmark) and trim mat corners. Mount light green triangles beneath each mat corner. For title words, adhere letter stickers to white paper and trim edges with decorative scissors. Mat with light green paper.

Kelley Blondin, Grand Blanc, Michigan

Snuggle Your Daddy

SHOWCASE A TENDER MOMENT

Amy's page features a favorite father-son snapshot. Create the border by trimming red strips with decorative scissors; mount along top and left edges of background paper (MPR Assoc.–paper discontinued). Mount ⅜" strip of striped paper (Provo Craft) along top edge. Mat photo with red paper; mat again with striped paper. Cut and mat hearts using red and striped paper. Draw black line accents. Adhere gold letters (Making Memories) to red paper and cut out. Write remaining title letters with red pen.

Amy Giacomelli, Monrovia, California

mackenzie, 6 mos.

PHOTO KALEIDOSCOPES

Photo kaleidoscopes are made by using multiples of both the original and the reversed (or mirrored) image of a photo. Cutting these photos on an angle and piecing them together again will give you a dramatic kaleidoscopic design.

For best results, select a photo that has vivid colors, good light quality, lots of activity, repetitive patterns or intersecting lines. For more on creating photo kaleidoscopes, see *Memory Makers Photo Kaleidoscopes™*. (See page 127 for more information.)

A Father

MAKE A PHOTO KALEIDOSCOPE

Donna's photo of her husband and son captures a touching moment that creates an endearing photo kaleidoscope. To make your own photo kaleidoscope, first mount background paper of choice. Then follow the directions at right; trim to frame photo and mount. Mat a favorite poem (as Donna did), photo or other artwork; mount in center.

Donna Pittard, Kingwood, Texas

1 *For a 12 x 12" page, start with four regular and four reversed-image (made by photo lab, printed from flipped negative) photos. Place a clear, 45° triangle on one photo to determine cutting lines. Move it around until the part of the picture you wish to use is visible beneath the triangle (Figure 1). Find three distinct reference points on the photo, which fall along the edges of the triangle. You will cut through these exact points on each original and on each reversed-image photo.*

2 *Line up your triangle to match the three pre-selected reference points on each photo. With a craft knife, cut the photo using your triangle as the straight edge. Repeat exact cut on the seven remaining photos (Figure 2).*

3 *Using one cut piece from a regular photo and one from a reversed-image photo, place cut sides together, matching them into mirror-imaged pairs along your predetermined reference points. Secure with removable tape. Repeat with all pairs of photos; assemble into page border matching all reference points. Trim center opening to frame poem, photo or other artwork; mount (Figure 3).*

Note: For an interesting variation, see page 113 for how to make photo kaleidoscope mats.

Daddy's Little Princess

CRAFT A ROYAL PAGE

Paper piecing and punch art helped Christiane savor this father-daughter moment. Print title and mat with pink. Punch large flowers and small circles. Layer on photo mats; adhere photos. Freehand cut crowns from gold glittery paper (Sandylion), blonde hair and dresses from floral paper (source unknown). Punch large and small flesh hearts for body. Punch large and small circles for faces. Draw faces with black pen; smudge cheeks with pink chalk.

Christiane Wilson-Grove, Kirkland, Washington

1-2-3 Kids

WATCH A FAMILY GROW

Charlotte's thought bubbles humorously illustrate her sister's growing family. To re-create this funny page, mat photos using colored rectangles and triangles. For the numbers corresponding to each child, adhere number stickers (Creative Memories) to small ovals. For the thought bubbles, freehand cut cloud shapes and punch ¼" circles. Write thoughts and outline clouds and circles. Adhere footprint stickers (Creative Memories, Frances Meyer).

Charlotte Wilhite, Fort Worth, Texas

Big Brother, Little Sister

CAPTURE SIBLING BONDING

The birth of little sister Rachel made such an impact on big brother Ryan that Jill wanted to honor their special relationship. Start with a selection of sibling photographs; silhouette all but one. Freehand cut the title letters from blue and pink gingham paper. Layer photos with letters. Journal with blue and pink pens.

Jill Andersen, Marietta, Georgia

Little Sister Store

LAUGH AT SIBLING RIVALRY

A funny "sibling rivalry" poem aptly fit the result of Kelley's attempt to photograph her two daughters. To create the "store," mat photo with blue paper. Trim bottom edge of dark pink rectangle for roof. Layer stickers (Mrs. Grossman's) along bottom edge of photo. Print the poem on cloud paper (Hallmark) and cut into a cloud shape. Cut an additional cloud shape. Mat clouds with blue paper. Adhere sun die cut (source unknown). Journal and draw blue dots.

Kelley Blondin, Grand Blanc, Michigan

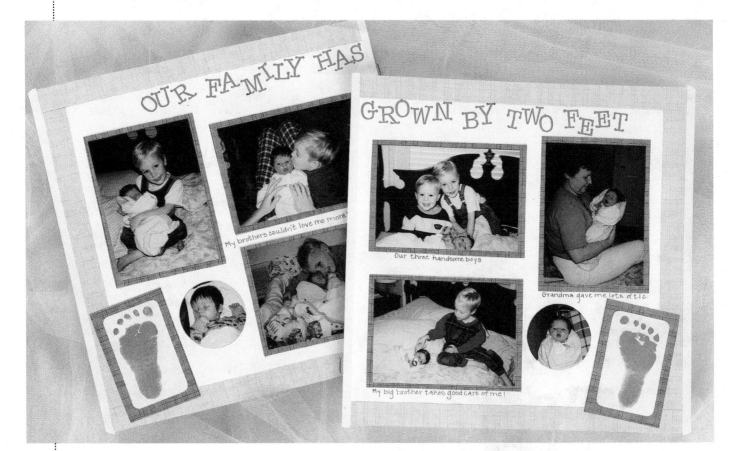

Our Family Has Grown By Two Feet

STAMP SOME TINY FOOTPRINTS

A catchy title and matching footprints highlight Laura's new-baby layout. For the border, cut ¾" strips from yellow printed paper (Keeping Memories Alive). Stamp blue title letters (Close to My Heart™/D.O.T.S.).

Round corners of stamped footprints. Mat photos and footprints with red printed paper (Keeping Memories Alive). Cut two additional circle photos. Journal with blue pen.

Laura Thompson, Spanish Fork, Utah

hannah, 9 mos.

my daddy does silly things with me

my daddy can touch his finger to the moon

He comforts me when I'm sick

My Daddy and Me Theme Album

FOCUS ON BABY'S ULTIMATE HERO

Ruth gave each of her twin daughters a storybook of her special bond with Daddy for a one-of-a-kind Christmas gift. The books' easy-to-read captions and the fun-loving use of stamps and humor make these storybook albums a perennial favorite of Ruth's family. Note how the photos selected successfully fit the limited scope of the book–My Daddy and Me. "The girls love their stories about what they did and how they acted as babies," says Ruth.

Ruth Freitas, North Dartmouth, Massachusetts
For more baby specialty album ideas, see pages 34, 38, 50, 73, 93, 103 and 119.

Sewing Album

Madeline Gordon, Orlando, Florida

Madeline made her tribute theme album, Nannie's Dream Stitches, as a Mother's Day gift in 1998. Madeline's mother, an accomplished seamstress, makes heirloom-style dresses for granddaughter, Ellie Claire.

"I had 'sew' much fun working with my mother on the dresses and putting together an album to document these priceless heirlooms," says Madeline. "When she received the gift album, she was nearly in tears and said it was the most thoughtful thing anyone had ever done for her."

Fabric: Polished Cotton 1½ yards at $9 per yard

Pattern: "Erin"

Size: 2

Notes: This was all Nannie's Idea. Ellie Claire wore it on her first birthday, April 3, 1998

Fabric: Liberty of London 1½ yards at $9.50 per yard

Pattern: "Margaret" smocking plate Creative sleeve arms smocked Needle 1997 Chery Thompson Pierce - smocked store Sharon view B length

Notes: I fell in love with this smocking date when I saw it on overalls in Creative Needle. I knew Nannie had some pretty blue fabric so she made it as a dress. One of our favorites. She also embellished a doll dress with silk ribbon embroidery to match.

As Ellie Claire's collection began to grow, so too did Madeline's desire to document her mother's handiwork by photographing Ellie Claire in her dresses and putting them in a special album.

Madeline uses fabric swatches from the dress as background "paper." Most of the dresses are hand-smocked with great detail and the extensive journaling about each dress makes this album a one-of-a-kind historical keepsake.

Ceremonies & Culture

All cultures have private and public celebrations to welcome babies into the family and the community. For your baby scrapbook album, save ceremony invitations and letters to Baby from loved ones to mark this special time when all commit to the care and protection of your child and all children.

Certificate of Baptism

DISPLAY JOYOUS MOMENT IN ELEGANCE

Donna chose elegant, laser-cut frames to showcase these precious photos of her twins' baptismal celebration. To make a similar spread, frame cream card stock background with ⅛" strips of taupe card stock. Mat baptism certificates on taupe card stock; adhere. Double frame photos with laser-cut frames (SDL Corp.); adhere. Add stickers (Mrs. Grossman's); journal with gold ink.

Donna Pittard, Kingwood, Texas

Alissa Rose

REPRODUCE A CHERISHED GOWN

(RIGHT) Teresa's paper-piercing mimics the smocking of her baby's gown. Add ½" strip of trimmed polka dot paper to black background. Crop photos; mat and adhere. Freehand cut dress, bonnet and name. Pierce dress and bonnet with a pin to add detail; layer around photos. Add journaling.

Teresa Quick, Cabot, Arkansas

alexis, 6 mos.

samantha, 3½ mos.

CJ's Dedication

PRESERVE A PRAYERFUL MOMENT IN TIME

Julie used photos of CJ's church dedication and journaled a special blessing as a reminder of God's love for him. Double mat ceremonial photo on blue and angel paper (Design Originals); trim with deckle scissors and adhere. Mat family photos on blue paper; trim with deckle scissors and adhere. Trim a 1" strip of angel paper with deckle scissors; place at bottom of page. Journal with blue ink.

Julie Staub, Loveland, Ohio

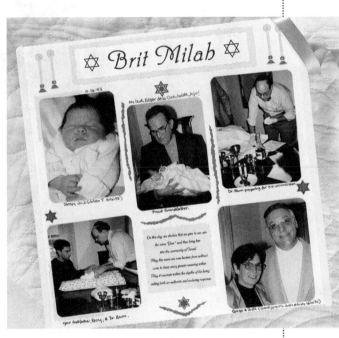

Brit Milah

CONFIRM FOREFATHERS' COVENANT

Annette's page commemorates son Julian's introduction to the Jewish community. Trim photo corners; adhere. Print title on white paper; trim with deckle scissors. Mat title on cream paper; trim with deckle scissors and adhere. Print blessing on cream paper; trim with deckle scissors and adhere. Finish with tiny strips of blue paper trimmed with deckle scissors and Judaic stickers (Creative Memories).

Annette Hilvitz, Overland Park, Kansas

The Blessing

CAPTURE ANCESTRAL CULTURE

Margie used a purple background, the color of royalty, for her page celebrating nephew Alec's traditional Japanese baptism at the landmark Meiji Shrine in Tokyo. Using purple lilac paper (Hot Off The Press) for a background, adhere double-matted photos. Finish with rattle and star die cuts (Hallmark) and journaling.

Margie Higuchi, West New York, New Jersey

Naming Ceremony

PRESERVE RITE OF PASSAGE

Kimathi Onome's first rite of passage was an ancestral naming ceremony performed by a priest trained in the Akan (Ghana, West Africa). The symbols on Sekile's page are taken from a symbolic language called Adinkra and from her own inspiration. To begin, crop and trim photos; adhere to page. Trim two 1" strips of tan card stock with deckle scissors; mount on outer edge of pages and add gold photo corners (Frances Meyer). Journal on tan card stock; trim with deckle scissors and adhere. Freehand draw symbols in gold ink. Finish with pen stroke stitching around photos.

Sekile Nzinga-Johnson,
Lanham, Maryland

kira, 8 mos.

Dutch Nursery Rhymes

RECORD FAVORITE LULLABIES IN NATIVE TONGUE

Dutch native Nicole and her husband sing Dutch songs to baby Destinee in an effort to raise her in a bilingual household. The scrapbook pages will help her remember these cultural melodies when she is older. To make a similar layout, mount red and white trimmed paper on a royal blue background. Draw ribbon border in black ink. Freehand cut flag and flagpole; adhere. Layer trimmed and matted photos. Layer double-matted, hand-lettered nursery rhymes and matted title. Adhere windmill cut from printed paper (Northern Spy) embellished with punched tulips. Add pen stroke stitching on windmill and flag to finish.

Nicole Ramsaroop, Orlando, Florida

Boys' Day

SHOWCASE CULTURAL SYMBOLISM

Every year, Jolene creates a page illustrating the symbolic significance of Boys' Day, a traditional Japanese holiday. In this manner, baby Brandon will grow up with an understanding of those who came before him. Start with a red background. Use Crayola® mini stamp marker to stamp yin/yang symbol on background paper. Photocopy "happi coat" kimono for border strips. Trim and crop photos. Double mat oval photo with red paper and kimono paper; trim edges with decorative scissors. Silhouette crop full-body photo; adhere with foam spacer. Finish page with journaling, arrow and target from kimono paper and origami koi fish.

Jolene Wong, Walnut Creek, California

Heritage

To know who they are, children must know where they came from. Babies' connections to their ancestors are biological, but their bonds to family are everlasting. Showcasing family resemblances and displaying your family tree and history will help your child find his or her place in the world.

• • • • • • • • • • • • • • •

Family Resemblance?

YOU BE THE JUDGE

Tracy color copied her and her husband's baby pictures to create this side-by-side comparison. Start by writing the page title with thick black pen on a tan background. Mat and layer photos. Journal with black pen.

Tracy Yonker, Alto, Michigan

Ancestors

PASS DOWN FAMILY HERITAGE

Along with a detailed genealogy, Linda included quotes from famous African-Americans about the value of family heritage. Print family tree (Family Tree Maker, Broderbund Software) or draw by hand. Print photo caption and quotations; mat with yellow paper. Mat baby photo with star die cut (Hallmark). Layer elements with star printed paper (Frances Meyer).

Linda Keene, Golden Valley, Minnesota

My Family Tree

DECORATE YOUR FAMILY TIES

Heather's drawings beautifully embellish the mats and bows tying together four generations. First crop and double mat the oval baby photo. Crop remaining photos into circles using a large circle punch. Double mat each circle photo with colored circles, ovals and rectangles. Cut bows from colored and gingham paper. Punch small hearts. Embellish mats, bows and hearts using opaque colored pens (Pentel Milky Gel Rollers). Title page and label photos with a thin black pen.

Heather Schram, Belgrade, Montana

Father and Son

COMPARE BABY PICTURES

Mary's son not only looks like his father but is also wearing the same blue velvet outfit. First mount a brown triangle on a white background, dividing the page in half diagonally. Cut photo mats using decorative scissors. Layer cream paper on upper left portions of two blue heart die cuts (Accu-Cut). Outline and draw stitches on all die-cut edges. Adhere die cuts and stickers (NRN Designs, Frances Meyer). Write titles and captions.

Mary Lisenby, Wichita, Kansas

When We Were One

COMPARE FAMILIAR FACES

Digging up old family photos helped Julie settle a family "feud" about which side of the family her son most resembled. For each photo, cut a tan and brown mat. Print and trace the Playbill font (Sierra On-Line) for the title words; double mat each word. Journal and write photo labels with black pen; mat with tan or brown.

Julie Gustine, Murrieta, California

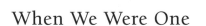

I Think That I Shall Never See...

OLD ART LINKS PRESENT, PAST

An old illustration of a ship helps link contemporary photos of MaryJo's sailor-suited sons to their ancestors' voyage to America. Begin with a navy background (Canson); add ¼" strips of gold paper at top and bottom. Photocopy clip art on cream paper; mount. Add navy-colored oval trimmed with deckle scissors above ship. Journal on vellum; trim with deckle scissors and adhere. Oval crop photos; adhere. Adhere matted title at top and bottom of page. Finish with embellishments (Creative Beginnings).

MaryJo Regier, Littleton, Colorado

Three Generations

FRAME A PHOTO LEGACY

Efrat's hand-tinted photos and museum-like framing of three generations of the Cain family is reminiscent of yesteryear. Use striped paper (The Family Archives) for background "wallpaper." Triple mat photos with gold, cream and burgundy papers. Layer gold frame (Sonburn) over photos. Finish with matted journaling and gold ribbon.

Efrat Dalton, Fort Collins, Colorado

meagan, 9 mos.

...ien, 11 mos.

Activities

While your baby's arrival may have seemed to move in slow motion, now that he or she is here, nothing will ever be slow again. You and your busy, busy baby will have many golden moments together: tender lullabies, fitful naps, splashy baths and eager feedings. Treasure every one of these moments, as well as the not-so-sunny moments of unforeseen illness and injuries. They, too, shall pass. Quicker than you could ever imagine.

SWEET DREAMS
MELISA THORNTON
MUNFORD, TENNESSEE
(SEE PAGE 126)

sarah, 12 mos.

Sleepytime

Nothing's as sweet as a slumbering baby. Capture these moments on film and record how you achieved them. Was it the blankie's satin edge that did the trick? A soothing lullaby? The security of falling off to sleep is a memory you will cherish and your baby will carry in his heart forever.

CLASSIC GOOD-NIGHT RHYMES AND LULLABIES

Lullabies help parents and Baby wind down at the end of the day and nothing sounds sweeter to Baby's ears than Mommy's and Daddy's loving voices in song. Some old-time favorites:

Golden Slumbers kiss your eyes...
Hey Diddle Diddle, the cat and the fiddle...
Hush, Little Baby, don't say a word...
I See the Moon, and the moon sees me...
Kumbaya, my Lord, Kumbaya...
Rock-A-Bye, Baby, on the treetop...
Sleep, Baby, Sleep, thy father guards the sheep...
Star Light, Star Bright, first star I see tonight...
Twinkle, Twinkle, Little Star...
Wee Willie Winkie runs through the town...

**SWINGING ON A STAR &
BABY BUGGY PUNCH ART**
*Tonya Jeppson, Boise, Idaho
(instructions on page 126)*

Twinkle, Twinkle Little Star

ROCK ON A CRESCENT MOON

(UPPER RIGHT) The stamps provided Cathy's design idea. To make the border, stamp and emboss blue dots and dashes, blue crescent moons and yellow stars (Stampin' Up!). Color stars and moons yellow and baby clothes blue. Cut large crescent moon and baby blanket from printed paper (The Paper Patch); layer with silhouetted photo. Add dimension to moon and blanket edges with Liquid Appliqué (Marvy Uchida). Adhere ribbon bows. Write titles in yellow.

Cathy Lay, Lake Zurich, Illinois

Sleeping Baby Quilt

SNUGGLE UP IN A QUILT PAGE

(UPPER FAR RIGHT) Jessica's photos lend the perfect focus to a baby quilt. Start by mounting photos in desired positions. Fill white spaces with colored and printed paper (Provo Craft) strips. Cut heart, star, flower and duck shapes. Punch ¼" circle for flower center. Finish with pen stroke stitching.

Jessica Fisher, California

The Story of Pooh and Twin

PHOTOGRAPH TREASURED TOYS

(LOWER RIGHT) When Cindy bought her son a "spare" Pooh as a backup, he soon needed both to sleep. For the page background, use yellow printed paper (Keeping Memories Alive). Double mat photos with soft blue solid and printed paper (Keeping Memories Alive). Cut soft blue mat for journaling. Punch Pooh bears (All Night Media) along the bottom of the mat. Write title, using the punched shapes for the "O" letters in "Pooh." Adhere Pooh stickers (Michel & Co.).

Cindy Mandernach, Fraser, Michigan

A Little Bird Told Me...

BUILD A COZY NEST

(LOWER FAR RIGHT) Barbara crafted this Geddes-style page for her granddaughter's birthday. Print the lettering and clip art bird directly on lavender background paper. Color bird. Freehand cut nest shape, trimming top edges with large oak leaf punch. Crumple thin brown strips. Layer photo and nest pieces with punched oak leaves and vine die cut (Ellison). Journal and draw details with black pen.

Barbara Parks, Auburn, Washington

Twinkle,
Twinkle,
Little
Star

Eric Joseph Wilkes

a little bird told me
there's someone new in
the nest......

...Jessica Lynn

.June·15·1991·

The Story
of
Pooh &
Twin

Justen got his Pooh bear from
Nana at his baby shower. He had
become so attached to Pooh that
we had to buy a spare. No store
had them anymore so I logged on
to the internet to see if the
company could direct me to a
store that carried it. They did
and we bought TWIN. Now Justen
is attached to BOTH bears and
needs both to sleep. He loves his Poohs!

Slumber Softly Little One

EMBOSS A POCKET-PAGE SPREAD

Heat-embossed celestial designs richly enhance Genevieve's pocket pages. Use 8½ x 11" tan card stock for background; layer with trimmed sky papers (Carolee's Creations). Silhouette cut clouds from angel/cloud paper (The Paper Company); adhere to pages at sides and lower edges, leaving top edge open for pocket. Circle crop photos; mat with gold paper and adhere. Silhouette cut angels from angel/cloud paper; mat with bronze paper; layer over photos. Stamp and heat emboss stars (Stampabilities), sun and moon (Rubber Stamps of America) and birds (Personal Stamp Exchange). Cut out; adhere. Journal with gold ink (Sakura).

Genevieve Glassy, Tenino, Washington

HEAT-EMBOSSED STAMPING

Heat-embossed stamping is an appealing way to add detailed illustrations to your scrapbook layouts.

To heat emboss a design, you must use a pigment stamping ink, which will dry slowly, allowing you to stamp several images before you sprinkle all of them with embossing powder. Embossing powders are available in a variety of colors and styles. Opaque embossing powders completely cover the ink with the color of the powder, so you can use any ink color. In contrast, clear embossing powders let the ink color show through.

To heat emboss a stamped image, follow the steps below. Be sure to keep your photos away from the heat gun or other heat source.

1 *Stamp the image with clear pigment ink. Liberally cover the designs with gold embossing powder (Figure 1).*

2 *Tap off the excess, using folded paper to return extra powder to the container. Gently sweep away any tiny bits of powder using a soft brush.*

3 *Apply heat with a heat gun until the ink "rises and shines" (Figure 2).*

Up All Night

REMEMBER THE WEE HOURS

(UPPER FAR LEFT) Susan recorded that unforgettable part of new motherhood–sleep deprivation. The pictures tell the story, so keep them the focal point with simple shapes and mats. For the window, freehand cut moon, curtain rod and curtains; layer with white strips on star paper (Creative Memories). Adhere letter stickers (Creative Memories) for title; accent with black dots. Journal with thick black pen.

Susan Gilmore, Orlando, Florida

Mommy's Favorite Lullaby

CHRONICLE A SOOTHING SONG

(UPPER LEFT) Sleeping baby pictures illustrate John Denver's "For Baby," a song that often calmed Stacey's daughter. For the background, mount gold and purple triangles in lower left and upper right corners. Print song lyrics and double mat with orange and star/moon printed paper (Colors By DESIGN). Crop and mat diamond shape for journaling and star and oval photos. Punch small stars and moons.

Stacey Shigaya, Denver, Colorado

Special Delivery

FRAME A NEWBORN BABE

(LOWER LEFT) Matching borders tie Kathi's theme page to her portrait page. For the page borders, draw scalloped lines using a thick purple pen. For the portrait, trim photo corners using a corner lace punch (McGill) and mount on printed clip art frame. Layer strips of printed quilt clip art around edges. Trim photo in envelope using corner heart punch (McGill). For stamps, cut and mat small photos, printed title, and printed clip art; trim mats with stamp scissors (Fiskar). For mailbox, print clip art and layer with silhouetted photo. Adhere small punched heart and floral clip art. Journal with black pen. (All clip art from Microsoft's® *Greetings Workshop* CD.)

Kathi Ivens, Truckee, California

Mason Garret Collins

PHOTOCOPY A TREASURED HEIRLOOM

To customize a baby gift page made for Mason's mother, Donna photocopied Mason's great-great-great-grandmother's quilt for background. Note that baby is sleeping on quilt in photo, too. To make the photo frame, quadruple mat with red, white and mulberry paper. Print title and trim with deckle scissors; mat with red paper. Adhere red ribbon bow.

Donna Leicht, Appleton, Wisconsin

COUNTING SHEEP
Freehand cut pieces; assemble.
Cathy Blackstone, Columbus, Ohio

Bathtime

Most babies have a love-hate relationship with bathtime, but it can be the most interactive and intimate part of Baby's and your day. When you can, bathe with your baby for extra bonding. And be ready to capture the giggles and tears.

Isaac

CREATE A PHOTO STAINED GLASS

Bobbie's page is part of a gift album she and her siblings compiled for their mother. For detailed instructions on photo stained glass, refer to *Memory Makers* Issue 5, page 55. To make the stained glass, cut the photo into an octagon shape. Cut the edges into a symmetrical pattern. Mount photo and "glass" pieces on black paper, leaving small gaps in between each piece. Extend the stained glass design using pieces of printed paper (Amscan, Hot Off The Press). Trim completed design into an octagon shape and mat with pink and black paper; center on blue background. Mount black triangles in corners. Label photo with black pen.

Bobbie Jacobson, Shaker Heights, Ohio

Our Little Stinker

TEAR A SWEET SKUNK

Torn paper adds a furry look to Linda's expressive animal. First mat photos with white paper and arrange on an aqua background. Layer black and white torn paper to create skunk. Trim thin white strips for whiskers. Draw eye and nose details with white pen. For title, punch white squares, mat with black paper, and write letters. Draw black and white line borders. Journal with black pen. Accent with yellow duck punches.

Linda Strauss, Provo, Utah

raelyn, 7 mos.

QUILLING

Quilling, an ancient art originally known as paper filigree, involves rolling thin strips of paper into various shapes and arranging those shapes into a design. Perhaps you made quilled art as a child. Quilling supplies are quite inexpensive and as you can see, quilling adds a fun and playful touch to baby scrapbook pages. The standard width of quilling paper is ⅛", but wider and narrower sizes are available. Besides quilling paper (Lake City Craft Quilling Supplies), you'll need glue and a slotted or needle tool. Rolling paper around the tool makes various shapes, while the number of coils made determines the thickness of the shape.

HOW TO ROLL QUILL SHAPES WITH A NEEDLE TOOL

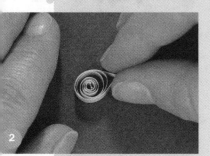

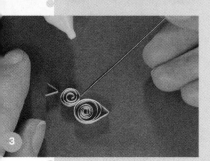

1 *Cut off a strip of paper to the desired length.*

2 *Slide paper strip into slot of tool and press the end of the paper around the tool with your thumb.*

3 *Roll the paper while holding the tool steady, keeping the strip's edges as even as possible (Figure 1).*

4 *Pinch ends, as needed (Figure 2).*

5 *Glue shapes together (Figure 3); adhere to page.*

HOW TO ROLL VARIOUS SHAPES

LOOSE SCROLLS: *Roll one end, leaving the other end loose.*

LOOSE CIRCLES: *Roll, remove from tool and let the coil loosen. Glue the loose end.*

TEARDROPS: *Roll and glue a loose circle. Pinch one side of the circle to a point.*

MARQUISE: *Roll and glue a loose circle. Pinch on both ends.*

TIGHT CIRCLES: *Roll, slip the tool from the roll's center and hold it to keep it from unwinding. Glue the loose end of the paper to the side of the roll.*

Bathtime Buddies

QUILL A SPLASHY DESIGN

Gail enjoys trying fun new techniques to enhance her scrapbook pages. Her quilled duck and fish designs can be a whimsical addition to any baby's bathtime page. To make this page, mount double-matted photos onto double-matted background. Use the quilling techniques described at the left to roll loose blue scrolls for waves; loose yellow circles for duck heads; yellow teardrops for duck bodies; large orange marquise shapes for fish bodies; small orange marquise shapes for fish tails and fins; and tight blue circles for fish eyes and bubbles. Glue rolled designs together to form ducks and fish. Adhere designs to page using tiny drops of glue. Finish with dot letter die cuts (Accu-Cut) and journaling.

Gail Birkhead, Tyngsboro, Massachusetts

I'm bringing home my girlfriend to meet my Mom and Dad. We'll laugh and have a good time, but then it will turn bad, when Mom gets out the Scrapbook when I was "oh

The Girlfriend Page

...so cute" and that first page that she will show is me in my Birthday Suit!

By mommy

Olivia's First Sponge Bath

BLOW BUBBLES AROUND FOAM LETTERS

Craft foam matched the sponge-bath theme of Tracy's fun layout. Start with duck printed paper (The Paper Patch) for page background. Round corners of photos; double mat using decorative scissors and gingham and polka dot paper. Trace title letters (Pebbles In My Pocket) onto craft foam and cut out. Mat yellow gingham duck die cut (Creative Memories); cut foam beak, black eye and wing detail. For bubbles, punch and layer different sizes of vellum circles, highlighting with white and blue markers.

Tracy Cabello, Granger, Indiana

brad, 12 mos.

Bath Time

DECORATE OLD-FASHIONED BATHROOM

Nancy cut checkerboard paper into square tiles to mimic her parents' 1940s bathroom. Start with a green background. Cut and mat circle photos and "bubble" for title. Cut white strips for chair railing and windowpane. Arrange squares of checkerboard paper for tile pattern. Cut pieces for bathtub, tub feet and window. Layer photo and stickers (Stickopotamus) beneath tub. Adhere additional stickers.

Nancy Chearno-Stershic, Bel Air, Maryland

Bathtime

SPLASH AMONG THE BUBBLES

The gray grout lines give Jacqueline's page a bathtub backdrop. After drawing the gray lines, cut faucet handles, spout and water droplet. Write title with thick and thin blue pens. Circle cut and silhouette photos. Layer photos with bubble stickers (Frances Meyer), duck die cuts (Creative Memories) and blue and white circles. Color ducks' beaks orange. Draw details with blue and black pens.

Jacqueline O'Beirne, Lake Barrington, Illinois

BATHTIME POP-UP

Pop-up pages are full of surprises, magic and fun. And best of all, making pop-ups is easier than you might think!

1 *Use a white 12 x 12" scrapbook page for background. Silhouette cut large bubble paper (Hot Off The Press); adhere to lower left corner of page.*

2 *Sandwich together one 8½ x 11" sheet of large bubble paper and one 8½ x 11" sheet of small bubble paper (Hot Off The Press) with right sides out; glue. Repeat with a second set of large and small bubble paper. Silhouette cut each bubble paper "sandwich." Layer together and adhere top of bubble papers to top ⅓ of background page. Fold up bottom ⅔ of bubble paper to form lift-up flap.*

3 *Transfer pattern on page 125 and center it on an 8½ by 11" sheet of white card stock. Fold card on fold line; cut on dotted lines (Figure 1).*

4 *Open card and carefully push out on the strips created to form the pop-ups (Figure 2).*

5 *Cover top half of pop-up with striped paper (NRN Designs) for "wallpaper" and bottom half with quilted paper (The Paper Patch) for "linoleum," trimming where needed to accommodate pop-up flaps (Figure 3). Lift up bubble paper flap and mount pop-up card to page.*

6 *Freehand cut bathtub and sink. Silhouette crop photos for bathtub; adhere to bathtub and add bubble stickers. Mount on pop-up strips (Figure 4). Add toiletry stickers (Mrs. Grossman's, Stickopotamus), placing foam spacers under bathroom scale, soap and some bubbles for added dimension. Trim a piece of old washcloth with fancy scissors for floor mat; adhere. If desired, make "puddles" on floor by using two coats of thick, clear embossing enamel.*

7 *Silhouette cut photos for front of pop-up card. Adhere to front of pop-up card, tucking under silhouetted bubbles where needed. Journal front of pop-up to complete.*

Rub-a-Dub-Dub

CRAFT A BUBBLY POP-UP

Pat's delightful bathtime pop-up page is complete with wallpaper, linoleum, toiletries and tiny "puddles" of thick, clear embossing enamel. Silhouette-cropped bubble paper and photos add to the excitement—even the family dog has a spot in the action! To make your own bathtime pop-up page, follow the instructions at left.

Pat Murray, Edmonton, Alberta, Canada

katie, 11 mos.

Grandma's Brag Book

CELEBRATE FIRST GRANDCHILD IN EXPANDABLE THEME ALBUM

Becky's mother lives 12 hours away, so when her first grandchild was born, Becky shared the moments in a "Grandma's Brag Book" theme album. The expandable album (Creative Memories) allows Becky to send her mother pages to "keep Grandma updated" on Baby's growth and activities. And even though the color theme varies from page to page, simple page treatments give the book its consistent look.

Becky Scott, Wenatchee, Washington

Mealtime

It is the best of times and the worst of times. The skin-to-skin intimacy of nursing gives way to the wonder of strained carrots suspended in midair. Labels from formula and favorite foods make great memorabilia. Photos of when mealtime is overtaken by sleepytime, as Baby nods off in the high chair, do as well.

Cheerios® Boy

POUR A BOWL OF FUN

Tracy's son stars in the cover photo for this cereal-box page. For the background, use bright gold paper. Double mat photo with gold and black paper. Freehand cut bowl, spoon and splashing milk. Cut ¾" tan circles for Cheerios; punch ¼" holes in centers. Freehand cut black title letters or trace from cereal box.

Tracy Yonker, Alto, Michigan

Cookies

BAKE PUNCH-ART GOODIES

Her daughter's love for cookies prompted Kathryn's mealtime photo shoot. To bake your own batch, punch and layer 1¼" jumbo colored circles. Punch ¹⁄₁₆" holes from Oreo cookie top. Punch ¼" brown circles for chocolate chips. Take a "bite" using scallop scissors. For pink cookie, trim tan icing with deckle scissors; punch small circle from center. Add layered die cut letters for title. Crop and mat photos and layer with cookies. Journal along border with thin black pen.

Kathryn Neff, Bel Air, Maryland

sara, 6 mos.

SWEET PEA

"I considered these photos 'throwaway shots' until I cropped them to remove a busy background," says Emily Tucker of Matthews, North Carolina. "I added them onto a hand-cut pea pod and now it's one of my favorite album pages."

Spaghetti and Meatballs

MAKE SQUIGGLY NOODLES

Alex's love of spaghetti was the inspiration behind mom Joanna's pasta page. Use wavy ruler to cut spaghetti strips; adhere. Crop photos with circle template. Mat with colored paper; trim with decorative scissors and adhere. Add fork die cut (Ellison) and extra "noodles" to complete.

Joanna Barr, Belmont, Michigan

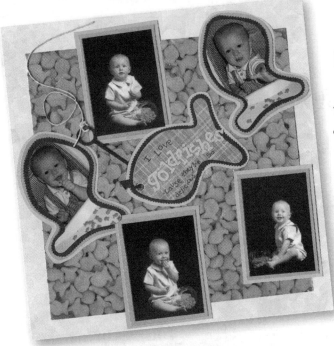

I Love Goldfishes

To match the theme of the portraits, Michelle color copied crackers in a plastic bag. Start by layering photocopied paper on a blue printed background (Provo Craft). Double mat portraits. Crop snapshots and orange paper into fish shapes; double or triple mat, trimming the black mats with decorative scissors. Write title and adhere letters stickers (Frances Meyer). Freehand cut hook and put through punched hole. Tie twine around the fishhook eye.

Michelle Gowan, Macon, Georgia

Too Pooped to Eat

CAPTURE A CLASSIC MEALTIME MOMENT

Rather than wake a sleeping baby, Michelle's husband made a pillow for their sleeping son. Use striped paper (Keeping Memories Alive) for background. Mat photos with white, checkerboard and printed paper (Keeping Memories Alive); trim yellow mats with fancy scissors. Cut title letters with template (Frances Meyer). Punch large white flowers and small yellow circles for centers. Freehand cut white flower and large yellow circle; journal and draw details.

Michelle Gowan, Macon, Georgia

jakob, 8 mos.

Logan's First Cereal

FEATURE YOUR GERBER® BABY

Mena replaced the Gerber logo baby with photos of her son. Start with a bright orange background. Crop and mat circle and oval photos. Next, Mena cut out and color photocopied cereal box parts and layered with smaller photos. Print and mat journaling.

Mena Spodobalski, Sparks, Nevada

HAVE YOU EVER SEEN A CUTER GERBER BABY?

Gerber

An excellent source of **Iron** for baby's first two years & a good source of **Calcium**

SEE SIDE PANEL FOR NUTRITION INFORMATION

Rich in Vitamin **C**

SINGLE GRAIN **Rice** CEREAL FOR BABY

LOGANS' FIRST CEREAL MAR. 22, 1998

BYGONE DAYS OF INFANT FEEDING

Long before Cheerios and Gerber foods were part of Baby's daily staples, infant feeding experienced a touching and often tragic past. While breastfeeding has always been essential for the survival of the human race, artificial or hand feeding has long been used when the breast would not or could not perform. Some interesting historical highlights include:

• Sheep, goat and calve horns are some of the oldest feeding vessels, readily available to hunters, gatherers and livestock farmers.
• Jug- and boat-shaped vessels of pottery and earthenware have survived from the Neolithic, Late Bronze and Early Iron Ages onward. Such vessels evolved into the feeding can, or Bubby Pot (16th century England) and still survive today as the spouted "sippy cup" used by toddlers.
• Late Medieval wooden, glass and other upright feeding vessels with screw tops and artificial nipples evolved over 500 years into the precursors of today's modern bottles.
• Pap-boats, used to feed pap or panada (gruel made from bread or grains and boiled water or milk), were used from the 17th to the 19th centuries.
• Sucking bags, the forerunner of today's modern teethers, are of ancient origin. Made of gauze or other thin cloth, these were soaked in pap or panada, squeezed of excess liquid and given to babies to suck.
• Nineteenth-century America saw the dawn of pediatric medicine, the scientific analysis of human vs. cow's milk, the campaign for sanitary milk supplies and widespread production of glass nursing bottles.
• The 20th century witnessed a decline in breastfeeding with the manufacturing of infant formulas and canned baby food.
• By the end of WWII, the U.S. Patent Office had issued over 230 patents for glass nursing bottles.

Twins feed from glass "turtle" nursers, introduced from England in 1864. They were commonly used for years until it was learned that countless infant deaths could be attributed to bacterial buildup in the bottles' feeding tubes.

Evenflo DELUXE

PYREX

Bugs & Boo-Boos

Baby's first year is generally healthy and happy, interrupted only by common illnesses and minor injuries. But Baby heals quickly with tender loving care from Dr. Mom and Dr. Dad, and these photos and mementos will help shape your child's sense of compassion for life.

Chicken Pox

ILLUSTRATE THE MISERY

A coloring book helped Bonita design this poor sick character. Start by rounding corners of photos and mats; layer on navy background. Draw and mat "fever" style title using thermometers in some of the letters. Cut and layer pieces for sick giraffe using printed paper (Paper Parade) for body. Draw details with colored pens.

Bonita Warren, Tillamook, Oregon

Emergency

PRESERVE MEMORY EVEN WITH NO PHOTOS

Cathy tucked get-well cards from her daughter's 1971 bout with croup into this medical-theme pocket page. For the top border, adhere line, letter and hospital-theme stickers (Creative Memories, Frances Meyer). For the pocket, cut a rectangle about half the size of the page and adhere along left, bottom and right sides. To decorate the pocket, mount polka dot paper along with a strip of white paper trimmed with decorative scissors. Outline with border stickers. Accent page with additional stickers and black dots.

Cathy Murphy, Downingtown, Pennsylvania

emily, 11 mos.

MEMORY WHEEL

Memory wheels are easily adaptable to scrapbook pages and are great space savers, using five photos at a time.

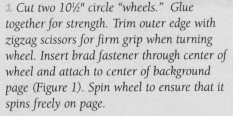

1 *Cut two 10½" circle "wheels." Glue together for strength. Trim outer edge with zigzag scissors for firm grip when turning wheel. Insert brad fastener through center of wheel and attach to center of background page (Figure 1). Spin wheel to ensure that it spins freely on page.*

2 *Cut five horizontal photos using photo pattern on page 125, positioning narrow part of pattern at bottom of photo subject. Mount photos securely on wheel with narrow bottoms surrounding center of wheel (Figure 2).*

3 *Use window pattern on page 125 to cut window opening 1½" down at center of cover paper that will cover the entire wheel. Place window opening over wheel, centering one photo in the window.*

4 *Lay window cover over mounted background and wheel; line up all edges. Use slot pattern on page 125 to mark slot for wheel on window cover paper over edge of wheel underneath and 1" from page edge (Figure 3). Slot should point to left if wheel will turn on left side of page, right if wheel turns on right side of page. Remove window cover; cut open slot.*

5 *Place cover on background; slide edge of wheel through curved slot (Figure 4). Adhere cover to background at corners and edges, without capturing any of the wheel. Journal about the wheel's photos; decorate as desired.*

The Big Accident

TAKE A "SPIN AND PEEK"

Chris uniquely turned a horrible double accident into a soothing memory wheel scrapbook page. She used two sheets of 12 x 12" red paper to encase the wheel and matted journaling, lettering (Provo Craft) and stickers (Frances Meyer) to finish the page. To make your own memory wheel, follow the steps at left.

Chris Peters, Hasbrouck Heights, New Jersey

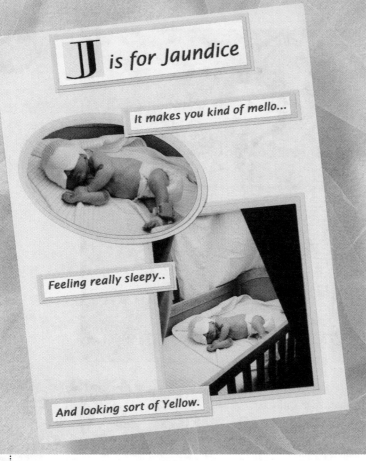

J Is for Jaundice

PRESERVE A SINGSONG VERSE

Nancy's husband sang these words to Hunter when he was hospitalized for low blood sugar and developed jaundice. Print the letter "J" using the New Yorker Engraved font (Print Shop Deluxe). Print remaining words using Lucida Sans font (Broderbund). Double mat titles and photos with soft yellow and blue. Layer elements on yellow background.

Nancy Kurokawa, Chula Vista, California

First Cold

SING THE SNIFFLE BLUES

Yuko's cute blue characters aptly express a head-cold mood. Start with blue checkerboard paper for the page background. Cut five doctor bags and layer using padded adhesive. Adhere letter and plus sign stickers (Creative Memories). Print and mat journaling. Circle cut and mat center photo. Cut two hot water bottles as mats for other photos. Cut and layer pieces for blue characters; punch eyes with ¼" round hand punch. Draw details with blue pen.

Yuko Neal, Huntington Beach, California

My Twelve-Month Check

SAVE THOSE BOO-BOO BANDAGES

Colorful bandages from her son's immunizations provided the idea for Cindy's Kermit® page. To make the frog pattern, Cindy photocopied and enlarged the bandage design. Cut and layer paper to build Kermit, outlining each piece with black pen. Mat journaling, bandages and photos. Adhere "ouch," bandage, stethoscope, syringe and doctor bag stickers (Frances Meyer).

Cindy Mandernach, Fraser, Michigan

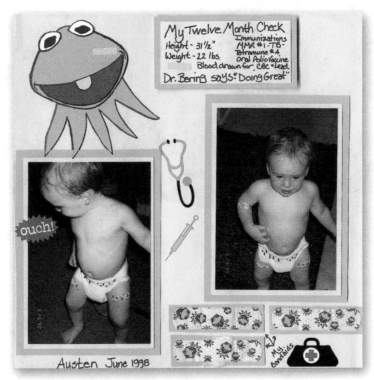

Day Surgery for Sara

DOCUMENT MEDICAL HISTORY

Kim saved the hospital ID button from her daughter's ear-tube surgery and color copied it for this page. Print the title and journaling directly on the page background. Crop and mat photos as desired. Label photos and draw details with blue pen. Adhere star stickers (Mrs. Grossman's).

Kim Owens, Lynnwood, Washington

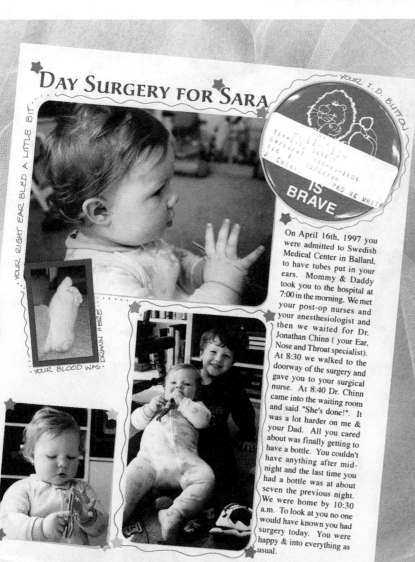

torin, 3 mos.

savanna, 7 ½ mos.

Playtime

PAT-A-CAKE, PAT-A-CAKE,

BAKER'S MAN

BAKE ME A CAKE AS FAST

AS YOU CAN...

Playtime may be fun for you, but your baby is on a mission. Behind those bright eyes and joyful giggles, little wheels are turning. Baby is learning about object permanence (peek-a-boo), word and action combinations (itsy-bitsy spider) and language skills (one, two, buckle my shoe). But more than that, baby is rapidly becoming a social butterfly. Preserve these playful photos, favorite games and baby nicknames while they are still fresh in your mind.

ariel, 7 mos.

BABY FACE
CHAR BEHUNIN
RUPERT, IDAHO
(SEE PAGE 126)

Our Little Olympian

PHOTOGRAPH A LITTLE GOLD MEDALIST

Inspired by the winter Olympics, Lesli posed these
cute photos for different events. Cut two blue wavy
strips and a 1¾" gold circle for medal. Mat photos and
printed journaling; adhere. Add journaling and
pen stroke stitching to medallion.

Lesli Erickson, Slayton, Minnesota

Chitchi's Story

New parents often marvel at the accomplishments of their offspring. Each "first" is greeted with thoughts of the genius we have produced. The same is true for Chitchi and Louis and their son David. But one activity worried them a bit at first.

"David would crawl away to amuse himself, and we would find him with a line of objects stretching across the floor," says Chitchi. "We asked ourselves, 'What is he doing that for?'" Other parents whose children exhibited similar talents later reassured them. "We've come to realize that it's normal, especially for boys," says Chitchi.

Some of David's favorite items to line up are CDs, books, magnetic letters, placemats, shoes and cars. David will often call his line of books his "train."

"He really takes after his dad's organizational skills," says Chitchi. "David has always put his toys away without being asked."

David has recently graduated to a higher level of organization. Previously he would line up all of mom's punches, regardless of size or shape. Now he sorts punches into distinct lines, separating the border, mini and jumbo tools into their own paths.

David doesn't line up things as often anymore, which makes Chitchi glad she documented his efforts on a special scrapbook page.

Chitchi Tabora, San Francisco, California

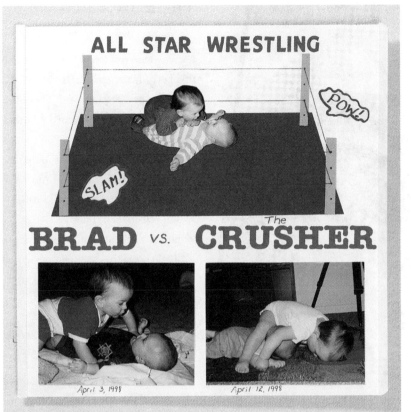

Brad vs. Crusher

FEATURE A FRIENDLY FEUD

Patti's humorous page captures the times her older son tried to show little brother who was boss. For the wrestling ring, cut navy mat and tan poles. Draw lines to enclose the ring. Cut free form white pieces for the words "slam" and "pow" and outline with thick black pen. Silhouette photo. Adhere small (Current) and large letter stickers (Creative Memories) for titles.

Patti Barnes, West Bend, Wisconsin

Next?

ENLARGE A MISCHIEVOUS SNAPSHOT

Liz scanned her son's pajamas to re-create the fabric's giraffe design. For the giraffe's spots, punch ⅛" and ¼" red circles; adhere. For title squares, stamp "Wasn't there, didn't do it" design (Rubber Monger), heat emboss and cut out. Mount giraffe and stamped squares. Punch ¹⁄₁₆" dots and mount around giraffe. Stamp title letters (Stampendous) in each square. Mat portrait with red paper and trim with jumbo deckle scissors (Family Treasures).

Liz Kajiwara, Palmdale, California

The Baby Patch

GROW A SUMMER PAGE

Cathie's embossed stamping highlights this berry-licious page. Use black paper for background; add ⅛" white paper border. Layer trimmed heart and matted checkered papers (The Paper Patch). Mat cropped photos; adhere. Stamp coneflowers (Mostly Animals), angels and fairies (Stamposaurus), sign (DJ Inkers), bunnies (Artistic Stamp Exchange) and berries (Son-Light). Emboss stamped designs; cut out and adhere. Journal sign and page edges.

Cathie Allan,
Western Educational Activities Ltd.
St. Albert, Alberta, Canada

So Many Names

PRESERVE BABY'S NICKNAMES

Kris and her family had so many nicknames for her son that someone once commented that Samuel might never learn his name. The words are printed directly on the background paper. To do so, use a computer to print the title and different names using a variety of fonts. (The page shown uses two horizontally overlapping 8½ x 11" pages.) Position the names so that they fit around a silhouetted photo.

Kris Morrison, Hastings, Minnesota

PEEK-A-BOO PIE

Scrapbook artists are continually searching for creative ways to use more and more photos on one scrapbook page. The peek-a-boo pie technique is a fun and easy solution. For another variation, try the Memory Wheel on page 79.

1 Mount berry paper (Frances Meyer) for background.

2 Cut one 11" circle (top crust) and one 10" circle (bottom crust) from tan card stock. Trim top crust using cloud scissors (Fiskars) to form pie's "scalloped" edge (Figure 1).

3 Transfer pie pattern on page 124 to top crust. Use a craft knife to carefully cut on all dotted lines (Figure 2). Scoring with a stylus will help create nice, crisp folds on flaps.

4 Adhere top crust to bottom crust; mount on background leaving enough room for page title.

5 Silhouette cut six favorite photos and mount beneath flaps onto bottom pie crust (Figure 3). Journal about each photo on inside of pie flaps. Add title lettering.

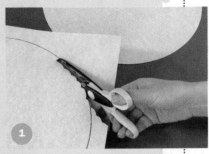

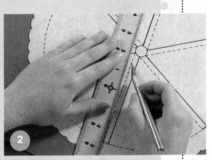

Cutie Pie

SHOWCASE PEEK-A-BOO PHOTOS OF YOUR "CUTIE PIE"

Kathleen's check on her napping baby girl brought the inspiration for creating her 12 x 15" "cutie pie" page. Each lift of a pie slice reveals a precious photo underneath. Kathleen's use of berry paper (Frances Meyer), cloud scissors (Fiskars) and red die cut lettering helps carry out the berry-licious theme. To make your own peek-a-boo pie, follow the steps above.

Kathleen Dodd, Dublin, Ohio

Couch Potato

An abundance of photos of her daughter propped up on the couch resulted in Amy's humorous theme page. To cut symmetrical couch halves, hold two 8½ x 10½" yellow rectangles together and trim three sides as shown. Mount pieces in a mirror image across the center of the layout. Draw couch details. Cut blue pillows and layer beneath silhouetted photos and white thought bubble. Circle cut two photos and mat with pillow shapes. Cut additional pillows for journaling. Outline title letters and color in.

Amy Paltelky-Flynn, North Muskegon, Michigan

100 Aker Wood Playground

PAINT A WHIMSICAL BACKGROUND

Hand-painted illustrations provide a storybook backdrop to Efrat's playground snapshots. First sketch tree and other elements around placed photos, outlining with thin black pen. Paint with watercolors. Adhere photos.

Efrat Dalton, Fort Collins, Colorado

Big Girls Do Cry

SHOW THE SUNSHINE AND RAIN

A photo shoot gone sour gave Carla the idea for this happy/sad page. For the background, cut yellow lightning bolt and sky blue and brown triangles. Crop and mat photos as desired. Use Print Master Gold software (Broderbund) to print large lightning bolt and small clouds with lightning. Freehand cut sunshine and additional clouds. Adhere umbrella die cut (Punkydoodles) and water droplet stickers (Mrs. Grossman's). Journal and draw details.

Carla Daniel, Bowling Green, Kentucky

Playtime

SPOTLIGHT ON FUN

Renee's page was one of her
first experiments with hand lettering. To start, freehand draw title
letters on green paper; cut out and outline with dark green pen.
Silhouette cut and mat photos. Layer photos and letters on printed
background (Close to My Heart™/D.O.T.S.).

Renee Sherman, Fort Collins, Colorado

Mommy's Work Is Never Done

MAKE A MESS WITH STICKERS

Cindy's border humorously illustrates the reality of life with baby.
Adhere border stickers to page edges. Add red wavy lines with a
wavy ruler. Layer furniture and object stickers (Mrs. Grossman's) to
create your own chaos. Crop and layer photos. Adhere letter stickers (Frances Meyer).

Cindy Mandernach, Fraser, Michigan

The Many Hats of Annie

LAYER A FUNNY FACES MONTAGE

When photographing her daughter in various hats, Molly often drapes the background with a sheet to keep the focus on the subject. After silhouetting each photo, layer on bright pink paper. Trim around entire photomontage, leaving a small border. Mount photomontage on a purple background. Journal with colored pens.

Molly Sheedlo, Blaine, Minnesota

Baby's Fantasy

PUT WORDS IN THEIR MOUTHS

An imaginative and funny page was Stephanie's answer for what to do with all those extra baby pictures. For the background, lightly sponge clouds, mountains, trees and grass using template (All Night Media) and stamping ink. Layer silhouetted photos with stickers (Mrs. Grossman's, Creative Memories, Sandylion, Paper House Productions, Michel & Co.) and other cut-out elements. Draw and cut out thought bubbles.

Stephanie Dueck, Whitehall, Montana

The Dreaded Dust Bunny

IMMORTALIZE A MISCHIEVOUS MOMENT

When her little ones had too much fun with the baby powder, Michele decided it was a Kodak moment. Start by cutting ¾" gray strips and four 2½" gray squares. Cut squares in half diagonally. Stamp and emboss winter daisy border (Close To My Heart™/D.O.T.S.) on strips and triangles. Mount triangles in corners of parchment background. Layer strips around each photo. Print story; trim story edges with decorative scissors and mat with gray paper. Stamp, emboss and cut out bunnies. Color pink bunny ears and cheeks.

Michele Rank, Cerritos, California

Even Angels Have Bad Days

USE UP THOSE "BAD" PROOFS

When Renee's normally angelic son decided he didn't want to be Cupid for his first Valentine's Day birthday, she made the best of it as well as this adorable page. Cut the title using letter die cuts as templates. Mat main oval photo with white paper; trim with decorative scissors. Arrange with other oval photos on colored background; trim edges with decorative scissors. Write title and journaling. Adhere angel stickers (Creative Memories).

Renee Belina, Apple Valley, Minnesota

daniel, 9 mos.

Pop-Up, Pull-Out Storybook Album

MAKE A POP-UP, PULL-OUT STORYBOOK FOR YOUR CHILD

Susan turned her granddaughter Bailey's love of books into a storybook for Bailey. The album is
full of little pop-up, pull-out, slide, peek-a-boo and wheel pages, always an entertaining favorite of young children.
The album's high-energy colors work well with photos of busy Bailey. Also included are photos of grandparents and
other relatives. "I wanted her to be able to see us when we can't be around," says Susan.

Susan Combs, The Chocolate Scrapbook, Louisville, Kentucky

kalen, 12 mos.

colby, 9 mos.

Recording Growth

GROWING INCH BY INCH

AND SMILE BY SMILE, BABY

STAYS LITTLE JUST

A SHORT WHILE...

Babies come into the world fragile and defenseless and emerge from infancy a year later as a strong and independent toddler. In her first year, your baby will likely triple her birth weight, learn to convey her likes and dislikes and acquire the roots of language. She will also learn to turn over, sit up, crawl and perhaps walk. And she realizes she is separate from you. Your child may never change and grow so much in a single year again. Keep a pad and pencil handy and take lots of photos to capture all of these once-in-a-lifetime events.

zachary, 12 mos.

PLANT A LITTLE LOVE
CYNTHIA CASTELLUCCIO
CARROLLTON, VIRGINIA
(SEE PAGE 126)

Aidan's 1st Shoes

CUT OUT PHOTO FOOTPRINTS

Ellen cleverly traced around her son's shoes to help record his first steps. To make the path, diagonally piece 5½" light gray strips on a green background. Adhere grass stickers (Mrs. Grossman's) along edge of path. Freehand cut dark gray pebbles to fit on the path. Make a template from a baby shoe to crop the photos. Deckle trim brown photo mats. Tear and crumple brown paper for journaling to look like a piece of trash for the ants to carry away. Adhere ant stickers (Provo Craft).

Ellen Underhill, Seattle, Washington

My First Haircut

BUILD BARBER POLE BORDERS

After five homemade haircuts, Kim took her son to the barbershop. To make the barber's pole borders, use a wavy ruler to draw parallel wavy lines about ½" apart on red and blue paper. Cut two blue and two red wavy strips. Intertwine a red and blue strip for each border. Cut gray rectangles for the tops and bottoms and connect with black lines. Crop and mat circle, oval and octagonal photos using decorative scissors. Place hair in memorabilia pocket (3L Corp.). Adhere haircut-theme stickers (Frances Meyer).

Kim Penrod, Overland Park, Kansas

BABY'S MILESTONE MEMORIES

Your baby's infancy will be packed with important "firsts." While it may sound like a lot of work to photograph and record these incidents, you will never regret it. Be on the lookout for the following milestones to enhance your baby's scrapbook album:

- *Clapping*
- *Crawling*
- *Drinks from cup*
- *First bath*
- *First birthday*
- *First haircut*
- *First holidays*
- *First illness*
- *First laugh*
- *First outing*
- *First smile*

- *First solid food*
- *First steps*
- *First tooth*
- *First words*
- *Lifts head*
- *Pulling self up*
- *Reaches for objects*
- *Rolling over*
- *Sitting up*
- *Standing*
- *Waving*

ANGEL BABY

To turn your baby into an angel, silhouette photo; add hand-cut halo and wings.
Pam Joutras, Lincoln, Nebraska

Monopoly

COVER THE FIRST YEAR HIGHLIGHTS

The spaces on Kathleen's Monopoly® board summarize her son's growth milestones and family events during his first year. Start by drawing the game board outlines with thick black pen. Label and decorate spaces for first year's events using stickers (Mrs. Grossman's, Colorbök), cutout shapes, punches and colored pens. Crop and mat photos, matching the mat colors to the board spaces. Adhere letter stickers (Creative Memories) for title.

Kathleen Fritz, St. Charles, Missouri

Meghan's Milestones

RECORD PHYSICAL PROGRESS

Ellen's "road to success" highlights her daughter's milestones
from crawling to walking. White dots add even more dimension. To complete the background, cut a yellow sun, green
grass and black road, layering as shown. Draw road and sun
details with a yellow opaque marker. Cut gray stones and
layer with silhouetted photos. Adhere flower (Mrs.
Grossman's) and insect (Michel & Co.) stickers. Add title
stickers (Making Memories); outline with white opaque pen.
Journal and draw details.

Ellen Miller, Syracuse, New York

The Baby Boy Who Could

RIDE A GROWING-UP TRAIN

(BOTTOM RIGHT) Jennifer built the photo moun-
tain by piecing photos together and cutting the
top edge. For the train track, layer small brown
rectangles on a thick black line. Silhouette
photos and layer with the train die cuts (Ellison)
along with black and colored circles and strips.
Cut various sizes of light blue clouds. Adhere
letters stickers (Frances Meyer) for the title and
journal with black pen.

Jennifer Brookover, San Antonio, Texas

First Airplane Ride

CONTAIN EVENT WITH EASY BORDER

Bamber's page commemorates not only moving from Paris to the United States, but also surviving an international plane ride with an infant. Start by mounting photos and airplane die cut (Creative Memories). Print title letters in an open faced font. Cut out title letters, mat with blue, and color in yellow. Adhere airplane stickers (Mrs. Grossman's).

Bamber Grady, Fort Hood, Texas

Growth Spurt

SHOW A YEAR OF SMILES

Circle photos and just two paper colors keeps Linda's layout simple to document progress. To make the title, adhere letter (Creative Memories) and toy (Hallmark) stickers to white paper strip; mat with light green paper. Crop and mat photos. Print, cut out and mat growth chart and photo labels. Arrange elements on page with rattle die cut (Creative Memories). Accent with additional toy stickers.

Linda Keene, Golden Valley, Minnesota

Watch Me Grow

SEE THE TRANSFORMATION

Mary labeled her pictures by putting a sign in each monthly photo. Use bear and swirl printed paper (Design Originals) for background. Round corners of photos; mat and adhere. Print title using the Market font (Microsoft). Adhere die cuts (Colorbök).

Mary Hortin, Albion, Illinois

Aidan's Teeth

DESIGN A DENTAL BORDER

Ellen scanned the tooth chart from a baby book and changed the colors to match her page. To complete the chart, deckle cut black and white mats and cut a pink oval for the center. For the border, cut pink gums with a scallop ruler and round corners of white rectangles for teeth. Circle cut photos. Double mat the larger photos with white and pink, trimming the white mats with notch scissors (Fiskars). Draw and mat title and adhere toothbrush and toothpaste stickers (Mrs. Grossman's). Journal on the dental chart and write photo captions. Layer page elements on a black background.

Ellen Underhill, Seattle, Washington

Hannah's First Birthday

CREATE A BALLOON BORDER

Marilyn created a classic birthday page using simple shapes and muted colors. For the balloon border, cut 10 mauve ovals using template (Delta). Trim crescents from three balloons and layer as shown. Crop and mat photos using oval template, corner rounder and decorative scissors. Cut pieces for cupcake. Punch small hearts. Emboss cake (Plaid) on lavender rectangle. Adhere candle and flower stickers (Mrs. Grossman's). Write title and draw details.

Marilyn Garner, San Diego, California

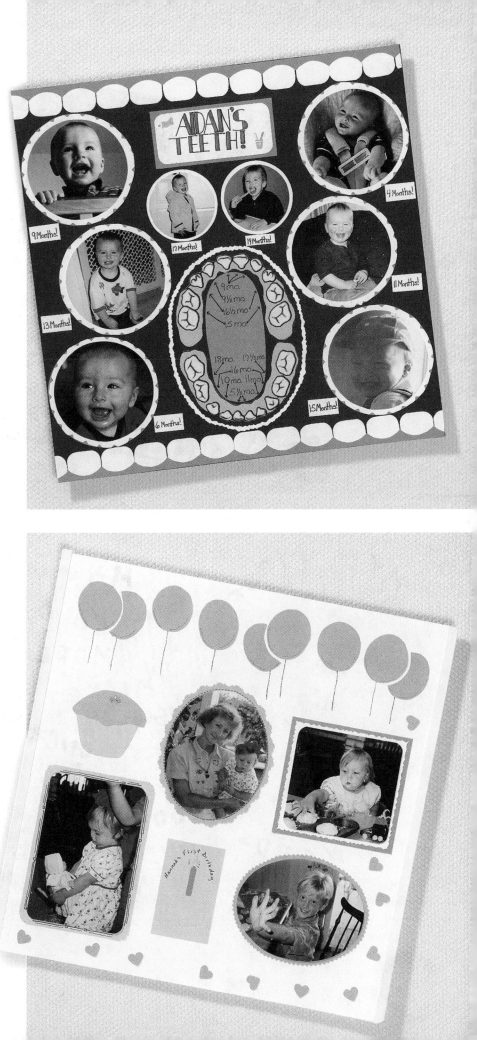

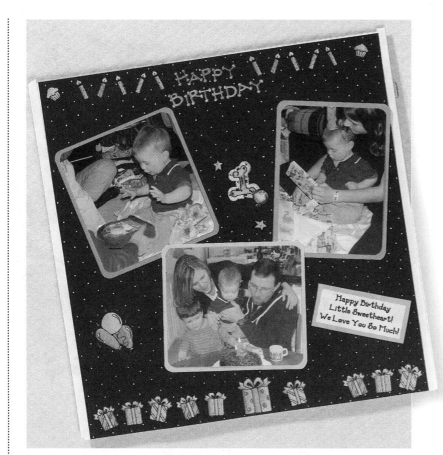

Happy Birthday

COLOR A CLASSIC MILESTONE

Cher colored her black-and-white birthday photos using SpotPen™ hand-coloring pens. To try out this technique, follow the package instructions to pre-moisten the photograph and apply the colors. Round corners of photos and mats and arrange on printed paper background (The Paper Patch). Apply rub-on cupcake, candles, letters, number, balloons, stars and presents (all Provo Craft). Print and mat journaling.

Cher Fudge, Wilmington, Ohio

My First Words

DOCUMENT BABY'S FIRST WORDS

Her daughter's growing vocabulary compelled Holly to create this vivid layout. Use patterned paper (Close to My Heart™/D.O.T.S.) for background. (**LEFT PAGE**) Mount large oval of patterned paper; layer with assorted paper scraps; adhere trimmed photo. (**RIGHT PAGE**) Double mat photos with patterned paper; trim with decorative scissors and adhere. Stamp words in red and black using Brush Stroke Caps (Close to My Heart™/D.O.T.S.); adhere.

Holly Johnson, La Quinta, California

Some just love to play outdoors Beneath the cool rain showers!

They start to grow the day they're born-- And some can get quite tall!

$3\frac{1}{2}$ mos.

Little Blessings

A story about Meghan Alison McCallister from birth to 5 mos.

...4 mos.

As little blessings grow and learn

They need a helping hand.

Little Blessings Storybook Album

RECORD BABY'S RAPID GROWTH IN A STORYBOOK ALBUM

In three days, Melissa made four of these charming "Little Blessings" books for relatives as Christmas gifts.
The book's theme, based on a Precious Moments™ book titled *Little Blessings*, helps share baby's good times with someone dear.
The album's photos convey the story of Meghan's first five months for grandparents and great-grandparents who might have
otherwise missed out on her joyful, daily growth. Note how the simple page treatments and captioning help draw
attention to the baby's photos. "The storybooks were a big hit on Christmas day!" says Melissa.

Melissa McCallister, Gainesville, Florida

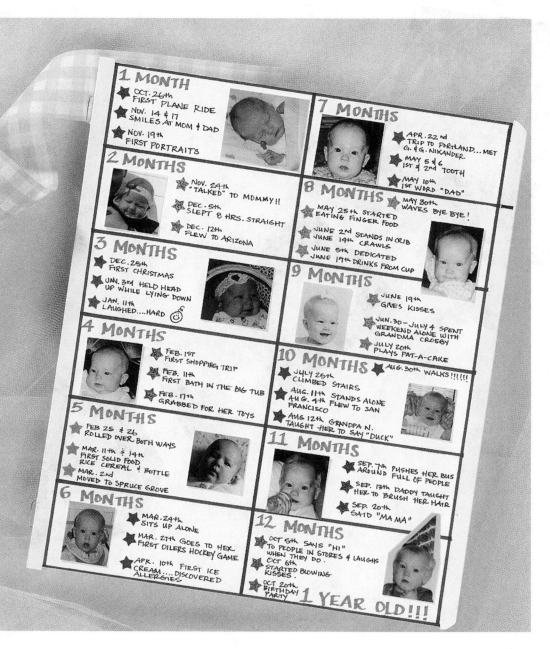

One to Twelve Months

SUMMARIZE WITH BULLET JOURNALING

Linda's journaling style is a quick way to cover a year's progress. Start by dividing the page into twelve equal boxes using a ruler and thick black pen. Crop and mount photos. Write month titles. Adhere star stickers (Mrs. Grossman's) and journal about each month's milestones.

Linda Crosby, Phoenix, Arizona

mason, 6 mos.

My First Year

GROW A CIRCLE OF LIFE

A softly penciled tree trunk provides the background for Kathy's vine of baby faces. First lightly outline trunk and branches. Shade with brown pencil. Use colored pens to write blue title and draw thick green vine. Cut out faces and mount in chronological order along vine. Adhere flower, butterfly and ivy stickers (Mrs. Grossman's).

Kathy Maggard, Edmond, Oklahoma

My First Home

REMEMBER HOME SWEET HOME

A square punch made it easy for Kathleen to build a brick house. Start by trimming 1" and ½" brown strips with deckle scissors, arranging as shown. Punch and trim cream and tan squares for bricks. Deckle trim black triangle for roof and brown rectangle for journaling. Crop and mat photos, drawing accents with thick brown pen. Mat cream triangles for photo corners. Write title and journal with white opaque pen.

Kathleen Fritz, St. Charles, Missouri

Sarah's First Year

WATCH YOUR BABY GROW

After completing this layout, Liza was amazed to see how her daughter had changed from a tiny baby. Start with green printed paper (Keeping Memories Alive) for the background. Cut square lace doily (Close To My Heart™/D.O.T.S.) into two triangles for upper left and lower right corners. For the upper left corner of each photo, trim the long edge of a lavender triangle. Round remaining three corners on each photo. Write title letters using purple, magenta and white pens. Journal with pink pens. Adhere flower stickers (Provo Craft).

Liza Wasinger, Fairfax, Virginia

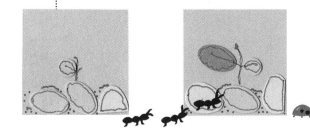
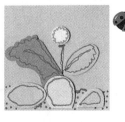

BUTTERFLY BABY

To turn your baby into a butterfly, silhouette photo; add hand cut wings and antennae.

Suzi Leverington, Narre Warren, Victoria, Australia

Calendar Girl

PIECE A TWELVE-MONTH QUILT

These pages are part of a four-page layout Kathryn displays using panoramic page protectors. For the title, adhere letter stickers (Making Memories) on gray background. Layer quilt design using square photos and colored and printed strips and shapes. For bunny (Design Originals *Punchin'*), punch medium and small gray hearts. Cut hearts in half for ears, feet and hands. Punch mini red hearts for tongue and nose. Accent each bunny with a monthly or seasonal theme using additional punches or cut-shapes. Journal and draw details and outlines with black pen.

Kathryn Neff, Bel Air, Maryland

kara, 9 mos.

lauren, 8 mos.

Portraits

A BABY'S PORTRAIT CAPTURES

THE ESSENCE OF SPRINGTIME

– ALL OF THAT WHICH

IS FILLED WITH HOPE

AND PROMISE.

GRIN AND BEAR IT
LINDA STRAUSS
PROVO, UTAH
(SEE PAGE 126)

A baby is truly a study in contrasts. Most times, he is covered with sand and strained peas, his hair in playful disarray. But for that brief shining moment in the studio, he is a beautiful vision in his birthday suit or Sunday best, his flawless skin scrubbed and every ringlet combed into place. Perhaps that's why we go to the trouble and expense to stage formal portraits of our babies, to capture on film the instant in which they really look in our hearts: healthy, happy, perfect. These special portraits command special treatment in your baby scrapbook album.

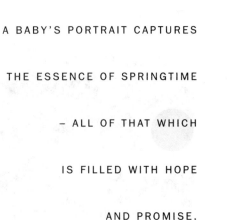

katelyn, 11 mos.

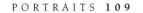

Hunter

PIECE A TEDDY BEAR FRAME

Tucking the photo corners beneath the hands makes Angie's bear appear to hold the portrait. Freehand cut the bear parts or photocopy and enlarge this page to make a pattern. Cut head, hands and feet from brown paper and clothing from gingham and star papers. Cut small pink half circles for the ears. Mat photo and layer with bear. Journal with black pen.

Angie Pitre, Kentville, Nova Scotia, Canada

Two Months Old

CRAFT A BABY BEAR

To add interest to simple portrait pages, Linda often re-creates photo elements such as this bear from her son's vest. Start by matting the photo with gingham paper. Cut navy triangles for the mat corners. Write and double mat title. Cut and layer pieces for bear. Draw details with black pen.

Linda Crosby, Phoenix, Arizona

TWO MONTHS OLD

AUSTIN RICK CROSBY NOV. 96

PRESIDENTIAL GREETINGS FOR BABY

"A congratulations card for your new baby from the president and first lady makes a wonderful scrapbook album souvenir," says Marsha Hudson of Seattle, Washington.

You can send baby's name, address and birth date to White House Greetings Office, Room 39, Washington, DC 20500. Sorry, no e-mail or phone requests accepted.

Zachary's First Portrait

FRAME THE SMILES WITH STYLE

Stacy's color choices are perfect for these classic little boy portraits. Start with a navy background. Print the titles on cream paper using the Party font (Microsoft Publisher); double mat with hunter and cream. Mount photos on cream mats using clear photo corners. Cut hunter green strips and layer around portrait as shown. Punch brown and green swirls.

Stacy Hutchinson, Whitehouse, Ohio

Eric

ACCENT WITH STRIPES AND PLAIDS

A monochromatic color scheme adds a classic appeal to Christina's portrait page. First border a solid blue background with 1" strips of striped paper (Keeping Memories Alive). For corners, mat four ⅞" navy squares with white. Cut oval frame from printed paper; mat with white and dark navy. Write names on oval frame background and in two corners using a white pen. Cut and draw "My First Year" banner. Layer banner and silhouetted photo with oval frame. Freehand cut first letter of name; mat with white paper; trim with deckle scissors. Cut 2" navy squares and printed mats for remaining letters of name. Write letters and draw dots with white pen.

Christina Storms, Scotch Plains, New Jersey

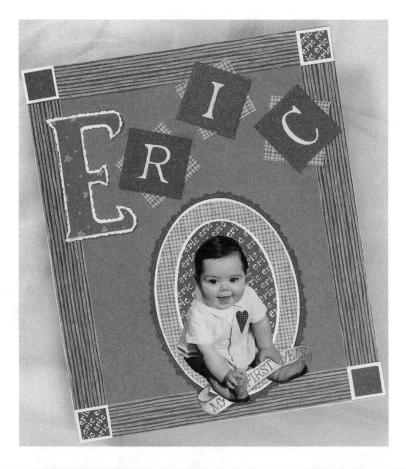

Seth

TAKE TIMELESS BLACK-AND-WHITES

When her son was seven months old, Tracy took photos of her favorite baby parts. For the portrait frame, cut a wide black mat. Write silver words and outline leaves and flowers; color in with colored pencils. Cut a slit around the design in the upper left and lower right corners. Tuck photo beneath slits. Mat remaining photos. Arrange elements on a gray background. Write saying (from *Naked Babies*, a book by Nick Kelsh & Anna Quindlen) with black pen.

Tracy Yonker, Alto, Michigan

caitlin, 6 mos.

Avalon

MAKE A FLORAL PHOTO KALEIDOSCOPE MAT

Carey enjoys making photo kaleidoscopes and found that a picture of her garden made a perfect frame for her adorable niece, Avalon. The striking garden photos successfully draw attention inward to the center photo of the baby. To create your own 12 x 12" photo kaleidoscope mat, follow directions at right; trim to frame photo and mount.

Carey VanDruff, Santa Ana, California

PHOTO KALEIDOSCOPE MATS

Photo kaleidoscope mats allow you to showcase cherished baby photos or create highly personalized gifts. For a polished look, the photo kaleidoscope mat should be created using a photo with colors that complement the center photo.

Making a photo kaleidoscope mat is easier than you might think, as you will see in the steps below. To learn more on creating photo kaleidoscopes, see *Memory Makers Photo Kaleidoscopes*™. (See page 127 for more information.)

1 *Select the photo you will use to create the photo kaleidoscope mat; have four original 4 x 6" duplicate photos and four reverse 4 x 6" photos made (Figure 1).*

2 *Using one original print, place the longest edge of a 45° triangle along the 6" side of the photo with the triangle point meeting a corner of the photo; mark the cutting line (Figure 2). Repeat with the remaining three original photos.*

3 *Layer one original cut photo on top of one reverse uncut photo and tape together at matching corners to create a mirror image. Place ruler over photo; cut on reverse photo. Now you have one pair (Figure 3). Repeat with remaining uncut three reverse photos to make three more pairs.*

4 *When finished cutting, mount all pairs onto page. Place another selected photo or artwork in the center and then frame as desired.*

Note: To make an 8 x 10" photo kaleidoscope mat, follow the instructions above using two original and two reversed-image 4 x 6" photos.

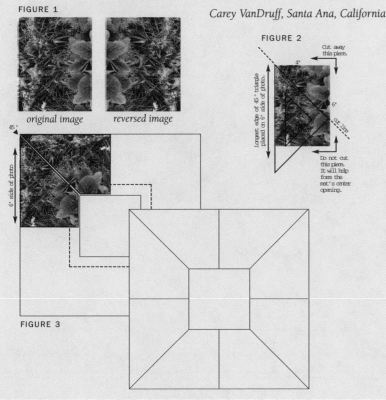

FIGURE 1

original image   reversed image

FIGURE 2

Cut away this piece.

Longest edge of 45° triangle placed on 6" side of photo.

Do not cut this piece. It will help form the mat's center opening.

45°

6" side of photo

FIGURE 3

Baby Girl

...down through a field of
stars & moonbeams, you were born
into this world, and the happiness
and blessed joy you bring to us is
more radiant than the sun and
older than the moon. The world
belongs to you Baby Kitty, along
with all our love.

Kathryn
Elizabeth
Pittard

8 Months Old June 8, 1997

Baby Fussie Bear, our boy born on the wings of hope and dreams, you are overflowing with the purity of innocence and all our promises of tomorrow. The world belongs to you and as you begin your journey, always remember how very much we love you.

Triston Michael Pittard

It's a Boy

8 Months Old   June 8, 1997

It's a Boy & Baby Girl

Stickers with a clear background (me & my BIG ideas) make Donna's pages look like custom printed paper. First mount each portrait on a colored background. Journal with silver and highlight with white. Outline page titles with silver and fill in with white. Trim and adhere stickers around portrait, borders and titles.

Donna Pittard, Kingwood, Texas

Cameron and Kyle

Leatha's monthly portrait sessions successfully document her twins' growth, while the large portraits provide an easy focal point for her cheerful page designs. For the "January 1997" page (LEFT), adhere line stickers (Mrs. Grossman's) about ½" from bottom edge. Draw red and blue vertical lines about ¾" apart using thick pens. Layer bear stickers (Michel & Co., Paper House Productions, Suzy's Zoo) over line stickers. Crop and mat photos, title and journaling. Trim mats with deckle scissors.

January 1997
~ 8 Months ~

Cameron and Kyle love to go to Aunt Lucinda's room and visit with her bears. They climb up in the chair with the bears then dump them on the floor and drag them around.

For the "6 Months Old" page (RIGHT), start with striped background (Frances Meyer). Triple-mat large photo with gingham, polka-dot (Frances Meyer) and red papers; adhere. Double-mat smaller photos and add red triangles at two corners. Trim title with decorative scissors; mat and adhere.

Leatha Ogden, Athens, Alabama

6 Months Old

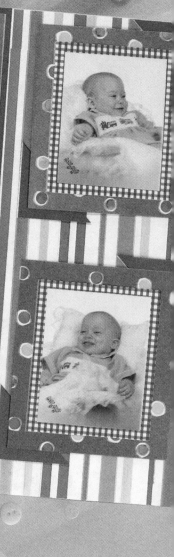

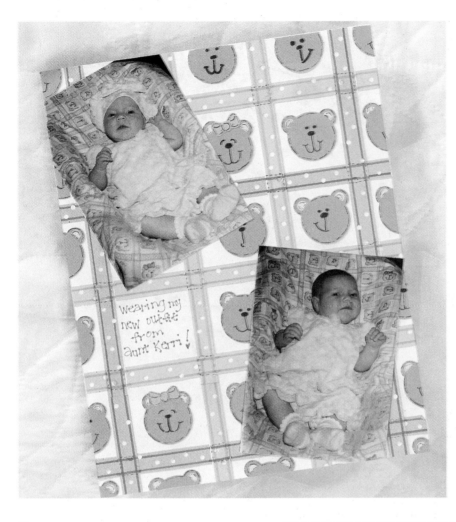

Wearing My New Outfit

PUNCH A "BEARY" CUTE PAGE

The blanket in the photos provided the inspiration for Kristi's punch-art bears. To build the background, randomly punch ⅛" holes from ½" colored strips. Arrange strips as shown. For bears, punch large circles for faces and small circles for ears. Punch ¼" circles for inner ears. Freehand cut bows. Draw faces and other details with black pen. Mount photos and journal with pink pen.

Kristi Loudon, St. Charles, Missouri

Becca

PIECE A PUZZLE PAGE

The Sunbonnet Sue design ties in the baby quilt made especially for this portrait of Robyn's daughter. First cut a small oval photo for the page center. Print journaling, adjusting the margins as necessary. Mat the journaling and a similar size white rectangle. Use an oval template (Puzzle Mates) to cut the center oval mat and trim the surrounding elements. Cut pieces for Sunbonnet Sue using printed (Provo Craft) and cranberry paper. To decorate the bonnet, punch small yellow circles and mini cranberry swirls. Draw details with black pen.

Robyn Dunkleberger, Ponca City, Oklahoma

Hey Diddle Diddle

CRAFT A DIMENSIONAL NURSERY RHYME

Large, whimsical design elements and a large silhouetted photo of Katelyn work in unison to bring a favored nursery rhyme to life. To make a similar 8½ x 11" page, start with purple cloud paper (Current) for background. Journal nursery rhyme down right side of page in purple pencil. Locate the patterns on pages 124-125 and then follow the steps below to make the design elements. To assemble, layer moon, cow, saucer, teacup, spoon and stars onto background, using foam spacers to lift the cup and stars for added dimension.

MAKING THE DESIGN ELEMENTS

MOON–*Transfer moon pattern to yellow card stock; cut out. Sponge dark yellow ink on outer edges to shade.*

COW–*Transfer cow pattern to white card stock. Using a thick dark purple pen, trace over all lines and color in spots and hooves. Color nose pink.*

CUP AND SAUCER–*Transfer teacup and saucer patterns to white card stock; cut out. If desired, trace cats along top of cup using stencil (Delta). Use a tiny sponge eyeshadow applicator to apply green, orange, pink and yellow inks as shown. Journal name on cup. Slit teacup with craft knife along front lip; insert silhouette-cut photo of baby.*

SPOON–*Transfer spoon pattern to blue card stock; cut out. Sponge sky blue ink on outer edges to shade (see below).*

STARS–*Trace stars using stencil (Provo Craft); sponge with blue and purple ink and cut out. (All inks used were from Paintbox2® by Clearsnap.)*

Hey! Diddle, Diddle!

The cat and the fiddle,

The cow jumped over the moon;

The little dog laughed

To see such sport

And the dish ran away with the spoon.

Once my knee made me sad

Or I can be elegant and dressy

My name is Katherine Mei Dawe

This is my family

Portrait Storybook Album

COMBINE PORTRAITS AND CANDID PHOTOS IN A STORYBOOK

Julie combined professional portraits and candid photos of her daughter Katie into a storybook. Punch art and stickers, along with the simple captioning and photo matting, give her little album its clean, crisp appearance.

"Katie loves to read her album because the story and pictures are all about her," says Julie.

Julie Dawe, Fort Collins, Colorado

PAPER FOLDING

Paper folding is a fun and unique way to embellish your scrapbook pages. With a few folds here, a few tucks there and some creative assembly, you can frame your photos with paper art that is reminiscent of ancient origami. And it's easy to do.

There are many different folds you can use. Here we feature the pointed petal corner fold. It's a great fold to use for experimenting with paper positioning. By assembling folded pieces in a ring, you can create a round frame.

Altering the number of folded pieces and the assembly method can yield square frames or smaller wreaths, with no openings, to use as embellishments.

For the wreath shown here, you'll need twenty-five 2½" squares (twenty-one for the frame and four for the corners) of lightweight denim paper (Hot Off The Press). One 8½ x 11" paper will yield twelve squares. Fold each piece following the steps below. Try folding a practice piece first.

POINTED PETAL CORNER FOLD

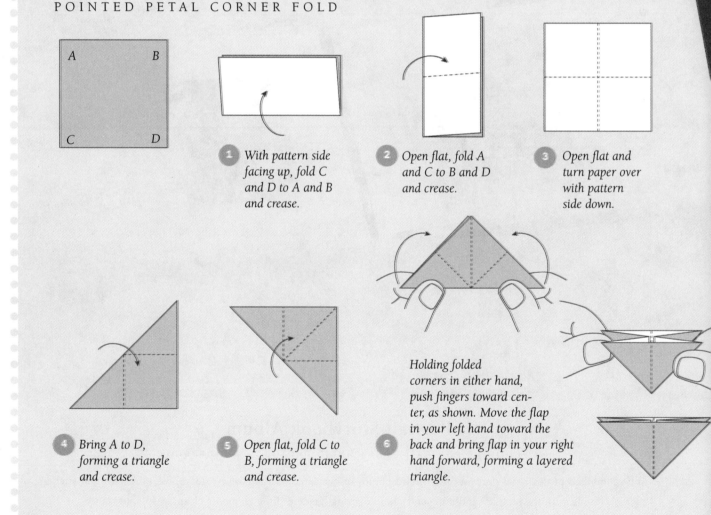

1 With pattern side facing up, fold C and D to A and B and crease.

2 Open flat, fold A and C to B and D and crease.

3 Open flat and turn paper over with pattern side down.

4 Bring A to D, forming a triangle and crease.

5 Open flat, fold C to B, forming a triangle and crease.

6 Holding folded corners in either hand, push fingers toward center, as shown. Move the flap in your left hand toward the back and bring flap in your right hand forward, forming a layered triangle.

jessica, 9 mos.

Paper folding technique by Kris Mason of Folded Memories and Laura Lees of L Paper Designs. Photo Cher Fudge, Wilmington, Ohio

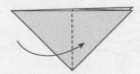

Brandon

The denim overalls on this adorable little guy inspired this denim folded paper wreath page. Begin with navy background (Canson). Cut twenty-five 2½" squares from denim paper (Hot Off The Press). Fold pieces following illustrations below. On separate sheet of white paper, use circle cutter to cut a ring that is 4½" on the inside and 5¼" on the outside. Use the ring and follow assembly instructions below. Place a 5 x 7" photo behind frame; trim if needed and adhere. Mount remaining four folded pieces at corners; finish with journaling.

ASSEMBLY

- Line up twenty-one pieces on circle's edge with even spacing and using the same reference points on each folded paper as shown below.
- Holding two pieces with closed points facing same direction, place flap of one piece into space between flap and diamond of the other.
- Snug up pieces so that the long open end of inserted piece is flush with edge of diamond of other piece.
- Secure with adhesive.
- Repeat remaining pieces, sliding first piece into last to finish.

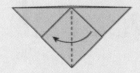

7 Bring top right flap to left side.

8 Fold top left flap down along centerline and crease.

9 Slide finger between remaining left flaps.

10 Bring top left flaps to right side.

11 Fold top right flap down along centerline and crease.

12 Bring top right flap to left side.

For more on paper folding, see Memory Makers® Memory Folding™. *(Ordering information is on page 127.)*

Lettering Patterns & Page Title Ideas

If you wish, use these convenient lettering patterns to add an elegant finishing touch to your baby scrapbook pages. Simply photocopy the lettering pattern, scaled to the size you need, and trace onto your page in pencil using a light table. Retrace and color in pen color of your choice. Or make your own patterns from the page title ideas listed by theme.

PRE-BIRTH
A womb with a view
Life on the inside
Showered with love
Twinkle, twinkle little star...how I wonder what you are
Under construction

Sugar and Spice and everything nice

a Star is born

LABOR & DELIVERY
A labor of love
A star is born
Baby's coming!
On the day you were born
Special delivery
Welcome little one
Your shining hour

Our little Angel

BABY ANNOUNCEMENTS
B is for baby
Heard the news?
It's a boy!
It's a girl!
Meet our new arrival
News from the cradle
Oh what joy, a baby boy!
Sugar and spice and everything nice
Welcome home baby

FAMILY
Brotherly love
Cuddles for Mommy
Daddy's girl
Daddy's little slugger
Daddy's pride and joy
Family ties
Grandpa's little princess
It's all relative
Like father, like son
Like mother, like daughter
Love my Grandma
Mommy's little stinker
Mommy's little angel
My heart belongs to Daddy
Our new grandchild
Proud grandparents
Sisters forever
That's our boy

cute as a Button

Grandpa's Little PRINCESS

TWINS
Diaper daze
Double delight
Double trouble
Seeing double
Twice blessed
Two by two

Special Delivery (LOVE YOU SO MUCH!)

DIAPER DAZE

born to be wild

Off to dreamland... Tiny Fingers, Tiny Toes

SLEEPYTIME

Angel baby
Good night, moon
Hush-a-bye baby
Now I lay me down to sleep
Off to dreamland
Rock-a-bye-baby
Sleep, baby, sleep
Sleep tight, little one
Sleeping beauty
Snug as a bug
Sweet dreams, baby
Sweet slumber

GOODNIGHT, MOON

CUTE AS A BUTTON

BATHTIME

Bath time makes life bearable
Bathing beauty
Best-dressed baby
My bath runneth over
Rub-a-dub-dub

bathingbeauty

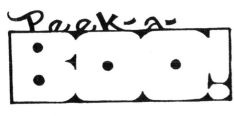

SOOOOOO BIG!

ACTIVITIES

Born to be wild
Busy hands
Feed me, burp me, change me, cuddle me
Fun in the sun
Hug me, squeeze me, love me
I'm on a roll!
Let's go bye-bye!
Look at me, I'm crawling!
Look, Ma, no hands!
Make a joyful noise
My first steps
Pat-a-cake, pat-a-cake
Peek-a-boo
Shake, rattle and roll
So much to do, so little time

HUG ME

SENTIMENTS

A baby is love
A blessing from above
A wee bit of heaven
Babies are a gift from above
Babies are a miracle of love
Babies are heaven sent
God's little lamb
Heart of my heart
Jesus loves me
Little one, you hold my heart
You are my sunshine
You are loved

MILESTONES

My 1st adventure
My 1st bath
My 1st Christmas
My 1st Easter
My 1st food
My 1st haircut
My 1st home
My 1st smile
My 1st steps
My 1st tooth
My 1st words
My 1st year

FINGERS & TOES

A perfect 10!
Our family has grown by two feet
Priceless parts
Tiny fingers, tiny toes

My 1st Haircut

PORTRAITS

Cute as a button
Lookin' good
Our little angel
Our little superstar
Sitting pretty
You oughta' be in pictures
You're so doggone cute!
You've got the cutest little baby face
Unbearably cute

GROWTH

Born to bloom
Growing by leaps and bounds
Growing inch by inch
How does our baby grow?
Inch by inch, growing is a cinch
SOOO BIG!
Watch me grow!

my first tooth

Patterns

Use these helpful patterns to complete certain scrapbook pages featured in this book. Photocopy and enlarge, as needed.

p.118

Pie pattern for peek-a-boo pie, page 87. Enlarge to 190% on a photocopier for 12 x 15" page, 145% for 8½ x 11" page.

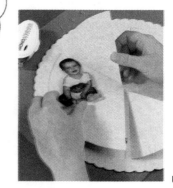

p.87

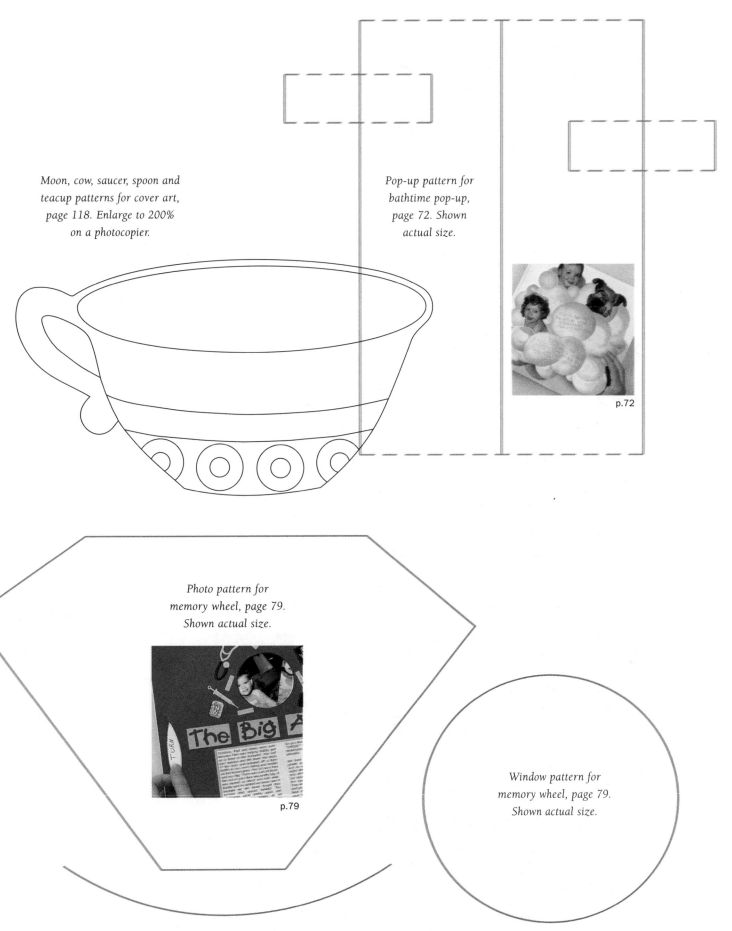

Moon, cow, saucer, spoon and teacup patterns for cover art, page 118. Enlarge to 200% on a photocopier.

Pop-up pattern for bathtime pop-up, page 72. Shown actual size.

p.72

Photo pattern for memory wheel, page 79. Shown actual size.

p.79

Window pattern for memory wheel, page 79. Shown actual size.

Slot pattern for memory wheel, page 79. Shown actual size.

cover photo
Katelyn Stephanie Barnard, Laguna Nigel, CA

title page
Cameron, 9 mos. Christina Husted, Kokomo, IN

page 6
Daniel
Use cream paper for background. Punch pastel papers (Canson) with large circle punch; adhere randomly. Mount photo. Freehand cut matted frame; adhere with foam spacers. Finish with matted journaling and ¼" hand punched pastel dots.

pages 10-11
Children Are...
Alex's button-adorned quilt spread is the perfect homespun layout for showcasing sixteen unrelated photos. Begin with teal background. Trim sixteen photos to 2¼" squares; mat with 2½" yellow patterned squares (The Crafter's Workshop) and set aside. Cut sixteen more 2½" squares from patterned papers (The Robin's Nest, Hot Off The Press). Randomly decorate fourteen squares with freehand cut and punched mats and buttons, using foam spacers under buttons. Journal last two squares. Assemble quilt, evenly spacing all squares ½" apart and ¼" from edges of pages.

page 12
Rhys Michelle Fletcher, Phoenix, AZ

page 14
Andrew Anne Detter, Dover, PA
Three Page Designs Artists were supplied with products from the following companies to create their pages: *PAPERS–The Crafter's Workshop, K & Company, Keeping Memories Alive, MiniGraphics, Paper Adventures and Royal Stationery. STICKERS–Frances Meyer, Mary Engelbreit, me & my BIG ideas and PrintWorks. STAMP–Uptown Rubber Stamps. 3-D KEEPERS™–C-Thru® Ruler Co.*

page 15
Kalen Jamia Bankhead, Lancaster, CA

page 16
Oh Happy Day!
Tamara's photo exudes her expectant joy over her positive pregnancy test, a great piece of memorabilia. Start with a sheet of textured paper. Cut another sheet of lavender paper into a starburst pattern; mount every other strip on the background. Double mat photo and punch large flowers and small circles for corner embellishments. Print and mat journaling. Cut out handmade title letters; mat and cut out each word. Print and mat journaling. Mount pregnancy test.

page 17
Wes Michele Rank, Cerritos, CA; *Jack* Mark Lewis, Denver, CO; *Emily* Heather Schram, Belgrade, MT

page 18
Paige Janelle Harris, San Rafael, CA

page 20
Joshua Jewelene Holverson, Pocatello, ID

page 21
Carlos Lara Janeen Lezcano, Pembroke Pines, FL

page 22
Annelise Renee Sherman, Fort Collins, CO

page 23
Derek Claudia Smith, Denver, CO

page 24
Introducing Jack Bayless
Katy's birth announcement was inspired by the story of Jack and the Beanstalk. For your own organic page, use decorative scissors to trim photo and background yellow square. Mount blue gingham paper. Mat photo and announcement with black and gold paper. Stamp green vines (Hero Arts) and sun (DJ Inkers). Adhere letter stickers (Frances Meyer), white fence and ivy stickers (Mrs. Grossman's) and bee stickers (Provo Craft).

page 25
Tori Wendy McKeehan, Sugar Grove, IL; *Kendall Drue* Lisa Elfstrum, Susan City, CA; *Marco* Kathy Medina, Carrollton, TX

page 26
Jackson Tricia Kelly, Thousand Oaks, CA

page 27
Taylor Claudia Smith, Denver, CO

page 28
Brenna Laurie Herlson, Butte, MT

page 29
Logan Shelley Price, Lakeland, FL

page 30
Mitch Joy Carey, Visalia, CA

page 31
Bethany Cindy Kitchin, Lemoore, CA

page 32
Mercedes Julie Trujillo, Thornton, CO

page 33
Jourden Barbara Wegener, Huntington Beach, CA

page 36
Tucker Alison Beachem, San Diego, CA

page 37
Katie Beth Ortstadt, Wichita, KS

page 40
A Baby's Body...
Deanna's love of classic black-and-white photos in natural light and simple embellishments give this page its timeless appeal. Adhere large photos to page. Crop and mat smaller photos on yellow paper. Freehand cut large and small daisies and leaves; adhere. Finish with pen stroke stitching and journaling.

page 41
Nathan Gerrie Kerby, Joplin, MO; *Alexis* Jill Aiello, Chatsworth, CA; *Nile* Jamie Getskow, CA

page 42
Alexis Lisa Garnett, Littleton, CO

page 43
Katelyn Stephanie Barnard, Laguna Nigel, CA

page 44
Mackenzie Tina Hall, Arlington, TX

page 45
Cameron Shawna Sanner, Des Arc, AR

page 46
Holly Kelley Blondin, Grand Blanc, MI

page 48
Hannah Karen Humayun, Timonium, MD

page 52
Alexis Tracey Carpenter, Baldwin, NY

page 53
Samantha Victoria Sherman, Apopka, FL

page 54
Kira Beth Smith, Auburn, WA

page 56
Doug Jeanne Ciolli, Dove Canyon, CA

page 57
Jason Linda Keene, Golden Valley, MN

page 58
Austin Jadelyn Alvarez, Folsom, CA

page 59
Amanda Nicole Donatucci, Ottawa, Ontario, Canada
Three Generations
Photos provided by Karen Cain, Denver, CO

page 60
Grandma's Heart chenille pillow and lamp Provided by Highlander Marketing, (800) 836-3810, wholesale only
Sweet Dreams
Melisa's page conveys her sleeping newborn's peacefulness with soft nighttime colors. Start by cutting clouds and stars from white, denim (Close to My Heart™ /D.O.T.S.) and yellow (Keeping Memories Alive) paper using template (PrintWorks). Freehand cut yellow moon. Mat stars and moon with white paper. Double mat photo. Layer elements on dark blue patterned background (Keeping Memories Alive). Use template (Pebbles In My Pocket) to cut yellow title letters; mat with denim paper. Journal and draw details with gold and navy pens. Tie bow with gold embroidery floss.

page 61
Darien Arlene Cano, Burbank, CA; *Meagan* Lisa Coultas, Lebanon, OH; *Sarah* Liz Dubenetzky, Carlsbad, CA

page 62
Andy Jenny Palamar, Kennesaw, GA
Swinging on a Star punch art
MOON & STARS–Lg. circle cut into crescent, sm. and mini stars. HEAD & TORSO–Sm. circle. ARM & FEET–Sm. oval. Freehand draw details. **Buggy Baby punch art** BUGGY–Lg. circle cut. HEADS & WHEELS–Sm. circle. WHEEL CENTER–5⁄16" round hand punch. HANDLES–Sm. spiral, negative piece from scroll border punch. HAT–Lg. bell cut. Freehand draw details. (For more baby-related punch art, see *Memory Makers® Punch Your Art Out Volumes 1 & 2*. Information, page 127.)

page 67
Katherine Julie Dawe, Fort Collins, CO

page 68
Raelyn Ellen O'Dell, Campbell, CA

page 69
Annelise Renee Sherman, Fort Collins, CO

page 70
Brad Denise Dawn, San Jose, CA

page 71
Hannah Karen Humayun, Timonium, MD

page 72
Katie Beth Ortstadt, Wichita, KS

page 74
Sara Kim Owens, Lynnwood, WA

page 75
Jessica Barbara Parks, Auburn, WA

page 76
Jakob Rebecca Goodrich, Missoula, MT

page 77
Alison Susan Brochu, East Berlin, CT; *Antique infant feeder and photo* Provided by Allen Morawiec, Littleton, CO, private collector and member of The American Collectors of Infant Feeders.

page 78
Emily Jennifer Wilkinson, Lynwood, CA

page 79
Maxwell Michele Rank, Cerritos, CA

page 80
Samuel Rebecca Goodrich, Missoula, MT

page 81
Jakob Rebecca Goodrich, Missoula, MT

page 82
Baby Face
Bright colors and a simple design highlight black-and-white photos of Char's daughter. For the border, write the "Baby Face" song lyrics separated by black lines. Crop and mat photos using bright colors and deckle scissors. Piece photos into a square design. Write title words on white strips.

page 83
Torin Michelle Fletcher, Phoenix, AZ; *Savanna* Pat Asher, Camarillo, CA; *Ariel* Lori Creamer, Belle Harbor, NY

page 84
Hunter MaryJo Regier, Littleton, CO

page 85
Andy Jenny Palamar, Kennesaw, GA

page 86
Quinton Cara Currier, McMinnville, OR

page 87
Amber Pennie Stutzman, Broomfield, CO

page 89
Jared Beatriz Boggs, Delray Beach, FL

page 90
Tucker Amy McGrew, Miamisburg, OH

page 91
Lindsey Denise Alford-Ray, Crofton, MD

page 92
Daniel Angie Ojeda-Kreiman, Fairport, NY

page 94
Plant a Little Love
When the photographer wanted to throw out the photo of her daughter sticking out her tongue, Cynthia told her, "No way!" Create a similar sunny page by double matting portraits using patterned (The Paper Patch) and yellow paper. Arrange portraits with rectangles of daisy paper (Geographics). Use black pen, decorative scissors and cream and yellow paper to create titles. Punch large cream and yellow flowers. Adhere raffia strips and bow.

page 95
Colby Cindy Browning, Chatham, NJ; *Kalen* Jamia Bankhead, Lancaster, CA; *Zachary* Michelle Peters, North Aurora, IL

page 96
Amanda Pam Klassen, Westminster, CO

page 97
Brad Denise Dawn, San Jose, CA

page 98
Camille Sylvie Abecassis, Denver, CO

page 99
Morgan Jennifer McInnes, Coarsegold, CA

page 102
Ashley Amy Talarico, Northglenn, CO

page 104
Mason Wendi Hitchings, Isaquah, WA

page 105
Ellie Wendi Hitchings, Isaquah, WA

page 107
Kyle Kim Skattum, Broomfield, CO

page 108
Fiesta Plush polar bears Provided by Summit Connection, (800) 777-1292, wholesale only
Grin and Bear It
Linda's freshly bathed baby and bunches of bears made for a perfect spur-of-the-moment portrait. First mat and mount the portrait; then draw a black line border around the page edges. Freehand cut thought bubbles for journaling. Punch white and gray bears and draw faces. Layer bears around portrait, using foam spacers for dimension.

page 109
Lauren Cheri O'Donnell, Orange, CA; *Kara* Pam Kopka, New Galilee, PA; *Katelyn* Stephanie Barnard, Laguna Nigel, CA

page 111
Morgan Cathy Shepherd, Santee, CA

page 112
Caitlin Dawn Mabe, Broomfield, CO

page 113
Dylan Holly Gressett, Springdale, UT

page 117
Trinton Lydia Rueger, Denver, CO

page 118
Rebecca Becky Burgeron, Egg Harbor Township, NJ

page 120
Jessica Barbara Parks, Auburn, WA

SOURCES

3L Corp.
(800) 828-3130 (wholesale only)
www.3lcorp.com

Accu-Cut
(800) 288-1670
www.accucut.com

All Night Media, Inc.
(800) 782-6733

American Tombow
(800) 835-3232
www.tombowusa.com

Amscan, Inc.
(800) 444-8887
www.amscan.com

Broderbund Software
(319) 247-3325
www.broderbund.com

Canson, Inc.
(800) 628-9283
www.canson-us.com

Carolee's Creations
(435) 563-1100
www.carolees.com

Clearsnap, Inc.
(888) 448-4862
www.clearsnap.com

Close to My Heart
(888) 655-6552
www.closetomyheart.com

Colorbok
(800) 366-4660 (wholesale only)
www.colorbok.com

Colors by Design
(800) 223-3130
www.cbdcards.com

Crafter's Workshop, The
(914) 345-2838
www.thecraftersworkshop.com

Crafts Etc! (formerly Stampabilities)
(800) 888-0321
www.craftsetc.com

Creative Beginnings (wholesale only)
(800) 367-1739
www.creativebeginnings.com

Creative Memories
(800) 468-9335
www.creative-memories.com

C-Thru Ruler Company, The
(800) 243-8419
www.cthruruler.com

Current
(877) 665-4458
www.currentcatalog.com

Delta Technical Coatings, Inc.
(800) 423-4135
www.deltacrafts.com

Design Originals
(800) 877-7820
www.d-originals.com

D.J. Inkers
(800) 325-4890
www.djinkers.com

Ellison Craft & Design
(800) 253-2238
www.ellison.com

Extra Special Products Corp.
(800) 648-5945
www.extraspecial.com

Family Treasures, Inc.
(800) 413-2645
www.familytreasures.com

Fiskars, Inc.
(800) 500-4849
www.fiskars.com

Folded Memories
(425) 673-7422
www.foldedmemories.com

Frances Meyer, Inc.
(800) 372-6237
www.francesmeyer.com

Geographics U.S.A.
(800) 436-4919
www.geographics.com

Hallmark Cards, Inc.
(800) 425-6275
www.hallmark.com

Hero Arts
(800) 822-4379

www.heroarts.com

Hot Off The Press
(800) 227-9595
www.craftpizazz.com

K & Company
(888) 244-2083
www.kandcompany.com

Keeping Memories Alive
(800) 419-4949
www.scrapbooks.com

L Paper Designs
(425) 775-9636
www.lpaperdesigns.com

Lake City Craft Co.
(417) 725-8444
www.lakecitycraft.com

Making Memories
(800) 286-5263
www.makingmemories.com

Marvy Uchida
(800) 541-5877
www.uchida.com

Mary Engelbreit Studios
(314) 726-5646
www.maryengelbreit.com

Masterpiece Studios/Royal Stationery
(800) 328-3856
www.masterpiecestudios.com

McGill Inc.
(800) 982-9884
www.mcgillinc.com

Me and My BIG Ideas
(949) 589-4607 (wholesale only)
www.meandmybigideas.com

Michel & Co.
(800) 533-7263

Microsoft Corp.
www.microsoft.com

MiniGraphics
(800) 442-7035
www.minigraphics.com

Mostly Animals Corp.
(800) 832-8886
www.mostlyanimals.com

MPR Associates, Inc.
(336) 861-6343

Mrs. Grossman's Paper Co.
(800) 429-5459
www.mrsgrossmans.com

Northern Spy
(530) 620-7430
www.northernspy.com

NRN Designs (wholesale only)
(800) 421-6958
www.nrndesigns.com

Paper Adventures
(800) 727-0699
www.paperadventures.com

Paper House Productions
(800) 255-7316 (wholesale only)
www.paperhouseproductions.com

Paper Patch, The
(800) 397-2737 (wholesale only)
www.paperpantry.com

Pebbles In My Pocket
(800) 438-8153
www.pebblesinmypocket.com

Pentel of America, Ltd.
(800) 421-1419
www.pentel.com

Plaid Enterprises, Inc.
(800) 842-4197
www.plaidenterprises.com

PM Designs (formerly Puzzle Mates)
(888) 595-2887
www.puzzlemates.com

Preservation Technologies, L.P.
(800) 416-2665
www.ptlp.com

PrintWorks
(800) 854-6558
www.printworkscollection.com

Provo Craft
(800) 937-7686
www.provocraft.com

PSX Design (Duncan Enterprises)
(800) 438-6226

www.psxdesign.com

Punkydoodles
(800) 428-8688

Robin's Nest, The
(435) 789-5387

Rubber Stamps of America
(800) 553-5031
www.stampusa.com

Sakura of America
(800) 776-6257
www.sakuraofamerica.com

Sandylion Sticker Designs
(800) 387-4215
www.sandylion.com

Sierra Entertainment, Inc.
(800) 757-7707
www.sierra.com

Sonburn, Inc.
(800)527-7505
www.sonburn.com

SpotPen
(505) 523-8820

Stampendous! (wholesale only)
(800) 869-0474
www.stampendous.com

Stampin' Up!
(800) 782-6787
www.stampinup.com

Stamping Station Inc.
(801) 444-3828
www.stampingstation.com

Stickopotamus
(888) 270-4443

Suzy's Zoo
(619) 282-9401
www.suzyszoo.com

Uptown Design Company, The
(800) 888 3212
www.uptowndesign.com

Westrim Crafts
(800) 727-2727
www.westrimcrafts.com

PROFESSIONAL PHOTOGRAPHERS

page 6
Daniel
Joyce Feil
Denver, CO

page 20
Joshua
Kapture Kids Portrait Studio
(800) 238-1195

page 26
Special Delivery
First Foto
(800) 443-0855

page 56
Family Resemblance
CPI Corp.–Sears
Grand Rapids, MI 49512

page 57
Father and Son
Heitz Photography
8008 W. 19th North
Wichita, KS 67212

page 64
Slumber Softly Little One
Diane Perry
5140 W. 120th Ave.
Westminster, CO 80020

page 76
I Love Goldfishes
Sears Portrait Studio
Macon, GA 31206

page 90
Tucker
Expressly Portraits
Beavercreek, OH 45431

page 92
Even Angels Have Bad Days
David T. Brown Photography
13800 Chestnut Dr., #215
Eden Prairie, MN 55344

page 94
Plant a Little Love
Lifetouch Portrait Studios
J.C. Penney
Hampton, VA 23666

page 97
Monopoly
First Foto
(800) 443-0855

page 109
Lauren
Ruth Clark Photography
20793 Valley Blvd., #D
Walnut, CA 91789

Kara
Sears Portrait Studio
Menaca, PA 15061

Katelyn
Lifetouch Portrait Studios
Laguna Hills, CA 92653

page 111
Morgan
Expressly Portraits
Foster City, CA 94404

Zachary's First Portrait
Moto Photo 533
Toledo, OH 43614

pages 114-115
It's a Boy & Baby Girl
Expressly Portraits
Foster City, CA 94404

page 116
Cameron & Kyle
Rogers Portraits
115 W. Washington St.
Athens, AL 35611

page 117
Becca
Cope Photography
202 E. Grand
Tonkawa, OK 74653

page 119
Storybook Album
Senger Portraits LLC
2190 W. Drake Rd.
Fort Collins, CO 80526

BIBLIOGRAPHY

Cone, Thomas E., Jr., M.D. *200 Years of Feeding Infants in America.* Columbus, OH: Ross Laboratories, 1976.

Eisenberg, Murkoff, Hathaway. *What to Expect When You're Expecting.* New York: Workman Publishing, 1984, 1988, 1991, 1996.

Emerson, Sally. *The Nursery Treasury.* New York: Bantam Doubleday Dell Publishing Group, Inc., 1988.

Fildes, Valerie. *Breasts, Bottles and Babies.* Edinburgh: Edinburgh University Press, 1989.

Hague, Michael. *Sleep, Baby, Sleep–Lullabies and Night Poems.* New York: Morrow Junior Books, 1994.

McKellar, Shona. *A Child's Book of Lullabies.* New York: DK Publishing, Inc., 1997.

Pfister, Marcus. *I See the Moon–Good Night Poems and Lullabies.* Switzerland: North-South Books, 1991.

WEB SITES

www.acif.org (The American Collectors of Infant Feeders)

www.ssa.gov/OACT/NOTES/note139/note139.html (Social Security Administration's Office of the Chief Actuary – popular baby names)

Index

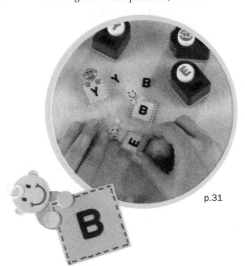

p.31

p.72

p.79